Business Networking for the Bewildered

Achieve business networking success right from the start and save yourself time, effort and money

By

Andrew D. Pope

LLYFRAU
CAMBRIA

Published in the United Kingdom in 2013 by
Cambria Books, Wales, United Kingdom

This book is dedicated to my beautiful wife Julie who is also my best friend and my trusted advisor

CHAPTERS

Introduction

Who this book is for?

This book is for anyone who wants or needs to learn how to build their business via networking.

It will save you time, effort and money.

If you are starting out in business and need to find prospects, leads and clients through word of mouth recommendations and referrals then this book is a superb resource to get you going effectively right from the start.

If you have been networking for a while but have seen little return for your efforts, this book will assist you in gaining a better understanding of the aims networking, identify and improve on your weak areas and help you generate more success.

If you are a well-established organisation that wishes to send employee teams out to networking events in order to build the business further, you would do well to ensure that they understand what is expected of them in order to achieve the objectives you set. This book will help them and it will help you.

It is sometimes difficult to promote an intangible service due to the fact that potential clients cannot see the "product" and may take more convincing to buy. Business networking, when done well, is a tremendous way to establish and promote your professional offering, build a solid network of referral contacts and boost your profits.

What this book is and is not about

This book is about face to face business networking.

It will give you all the knowledge you need to fully understand the aims and benefits of good business networking.

It will give you all the fundamental tools and techniques that you will need: to network successfully on an ad hoc basis, to network successfully at general business events, to select organised networking groups and events, to prepare for organised events, to be effective during the organised events and to purposefully follow-up after all of your networking activity.

It will also give you many hints, tips and strategies about networking best practice as well as what to avoid.

What this book is not about is online networking. It is not about getting prospects or connections via social media, e-mail, websites, blogs, etc... There are many excellent books available covering online marketing.

Whilst it is fair to say that many of the communication skills and techniques you will learn will be of huge use to you when dealing electronically with your contacts, this book does not aim to cover this area at all other than a mention about follow-up e-mails.

Personally, I prefer the old-fashioned "looking people in the eyes and shaking hands" style of communicating and networking. It is still the best way to get to know people well and for them to get to know you well.

Who am I to be writing this book?

I am a business owner. My work involves helping people and organisations develop more effective face to face communication skills. I am a speaker, speaker coach, trainer and I write extensively about face to face communication skills and self-development.

I am also a business networker. I understand how effective it is as a marketing tool because I use it to build my own business.

Business networking definitely falls under my remit as it is all about face to face communication skills. There are however many unique facets that can make it a tough challenge to get right, especially for beginners.

When I first started networking, I had no instruction manual to guide me and, although I considered myself an effective communicator, there was a steep learning curve involved. This learning curve has cost me much time and money through my many mistakes and wasted effort. I am still learning new things all the time.

Truth to be told, my first forays into the networking arena were an abject disaster. I came close to giving up on the whole idea due to the way I felt. I knew I had to go out and do this networking thing because, as a provider of intangible coaching services, I was actually the product. At first I had no clear business message to share, I tried to sell directly, I was frequently messed about by time wasters, I spent a lot of money I could have used for more productive business reasons and I wasted time by simply trying to connect with the wrong people. I found myself in uncomfortable situations where I felt like a fish out of water, shy and nervous and quite often rather stupid.

I was lucky with the second and more well-established network group that I joined. I was unhappy with my first selection so I spent a lot of time checking out various potential groups. I found it was difficult to say no to some of them, even if I knew they were not for me, due to the encouraging noises, offers and promises of fantastic membership quality that they made; I know better now of course. I eventually learnt a huge amount by talking to, observing and copying the better networkers in this second group. I finally figured most of it out to my own satisfaction.

I have now applied all the other communication skills I have learnt to the issue and built a workable networking strategy and a toolkit of techniques that you are welcome to use for your own rapid progress and success. Business networking now provides a large part of my business generation and I am continually building traction and momentum as my business relationships with others mature and grow. I would heartily recommend it to you.

I am not any sort of guru and this book is a guaranteed "guru-free" zone. I don't even consider myself an expert. I simply wrote this book on the basis that I would have benefited hugely from it when I started out, so others will benefit from it too. You will benefit from it. It is my sincere hope that you will save yourself time, money and wasted effort and go out networking successfully from this point onwards.

This is a practical book for busy working people. I aim to give you useable techniques, facts, options, opinions, challenges, choices and information on things that I have found to be useful and not so useful.

Structural overview

The subject of business networking will be covered in the following broad steps:

- What is business networking and why do you need it?

- The aim and strategy for good business networking

- Selecting where best to network and with whom

- Creating your business networking message

- Effective preparation prior to organised events

- Being highly effective at organised events

- Achieving effective networking follow-up

- Reality checks and performance monitoring

- Increasing your credibility by speaking up

- Ideas for effective control of a networking team

- Summary, final thoughts and some next steps

Each stage will challenge you and hopefully give you interesting insights about business networking itself and also the nature of your unique business offering and your relationship to it.

How to get the best from this book

Like all things in life, you only get out what you put in.

This book is no exception.

Networking is a highly practical subject. You cannot network theoretically; studying networking is not networking. You have to actually go out and network with actual real people in actual real places. If this all seems rather obvious then you might be surprised at how many people don't put the work in or don't go to enough events to be effective. They then believe that networking itself is ineffective or simply not for them. They are missing out.

Networking is definitely a skill that can be taught and developed and will more than repay the effort you put in.

I recommend reading the book right through initially, to get a feel for the overall subject of networking, then either concentrate on the various stages where you need more understanding or start from the most appropriate place, depending on your level of experience with networking, and work forwards from there.

For example, if I was a novice I would read the book right through then start again from the beginning and work through the book whilst practicing and building on each stage. Lots of practice coupled with a willingness to step out of your comfort zone will make you a successful networker.

As another example, if I was a more experienced networker who was getting poor returns, I would read right through the book first to try and identify potential problem areas then concentrate my efforts on these one at a time whilst monitoring for any improvements. Revisiting the reality check section and honestly answering the questions there may reveal some hidden issues.

Networking is like any other business activity. We need to monitor it and appraise it for effectiveness and return on investment. There is no point trying to fool yourself or carry on when you realise there is a real problem.

Try the things that make you uncomfortable. Discomfort means personal growth. You will get better and better.

Above all, remember to have fun at any events you go to. You will meet some fantastic people. I hope you are not in business solely to make money. Your quality of life and work life balance are vitally important.

I hope you enjoy the journey.

Chapter 1 - Business networking

What is all the fuss about?

Historically, networking occurred when you simply kept in regular touch with your friends, peers and business colleagues. You might refer them to work and they in turn might refer you.

How then does modern business networking differ from this?

The good news is there is no fundamental difference as networking, in both the personal and the business sense, will always be about building solid, quality relationships over time.

Traditional networking, therefore, still takes place between friends, family and colleagues the same way it has for years; the only difference being in the number of new ways that we can communicate with each other.

Although I will cover ad hoc and general business event networking, this book is primarily concerned with the modern organised forms of business networking which are becoming more and more popular these days. These forms are designed and run purely to facilitate networking activity between businesses of all kinds.

It is this kind of organised and specific networking that most business people think of whenever the term business networking is mentioned.

These modern forms of organised networking can be extremely beneficial to you and your business, yet it is also these exact types of business networking that can give people most cause for concern.

Some people struggle with the thought of having to meet many complete strangers and working the room. Some people struggle with the concept of self-marketing without being thought of as pushy or worse. Some people worry that it will cost too much for too little return. Some may have tried it already and found the whole experience highly unpleasant due to any number of possible reasons. The list could go on and all the concerns are real and fully justifiable.

Fear not, I will start right from first principles and guide you through the process in order that you can not only start, or resume, going to modern organised networking events but actually gain real benefits and enjoyment from them.

The term business networking has also been called referral networking, relationship marketing, business to business (B2B) referral networking, etc... They all mean much the same thing. To keep things simple I will refer only to business networking from now on.

The knowledge, skills and techniques you will learn here are applicable to all forms of face to face networking. Many of the general principles covered will also serve you well in your wider business life and your personal life. The ability to communicate well in face to face situations is an extremely valuable skill to cultivate.

Why do you need networking?

Whatever business you think you are in please be fully aware that you are also in the marketing business. You need to get the message out about your business offerings and you need to get that message heard. You need a steady stream of suitable business prospects in your sights so that you can present proposals to them and ultimately win business from them.

However, there is so much noise in our modern world, in the form of constant advertising in many media, that we are becoming immune to it all; we are developing the ability to tune it all out and ignore it. Bear in mind that your message will be just as likely to be perceived as noise and thus ignored by everyone else, including your target market.

Time is rare and more valuable than ever. Time pressure is always on the modern manager. The economic buyers of services are getting harder to reach. Getting even small amounts of favourable attention to present your service offerings is becoming ever more difficult. Dutiful and suspicious gatekeepers are constantly on their guard to deflect incoming salespeople and sales messages; thus protecting their bosses from yet more costly distractions.

What can you do about this?

Let me start with an analogy to get you thinking.

Think back to when you were buying your first sensible car. I say sensible car because you may need to discount your very first one which was likely an impulse purchase with little real thought placed on the potential downside. The first car I bought was sold to me by a mate and it was at the scrap yard within two weeks. I was down by fifty pounds, one mate and on the bus again. If you haven't bought a sensible car yet, imagine what it will be like when you do. Getting your first sensible car was a big occasion and was likely a substantial financial outlay. It was extremely important to get a good deal and a good vehicle. There were many garages out there and all seemed to have good offers and cars.

If you were like me back then you knew little about cars; I still don't I'm afraid to say. Did you risk taking pot luck and picking one or did you ask for advice and a recommendation from a trusted friend or parent?

If they were available, I'm betting you listened to all the advice and recommendations and in fact you welcomed them. They took the pressure off you, helped you spend your money wisely and hopefully got you a good vehicle.

A garage recommendation could have come in two forms: firstly, the person had heard that the garage was good and that other people had done well there or secondly, the person had used the garage themselves and been delighted with the results.

I don't know about you but, if I trusted the person making the recommendation, I would have gone for the second recommendation straight away and visited that garage for my car. This is actually what happened; I got a good deal and an excellent motor that lasted me years.

This is where networking enters the scene.

The basic idea is the same as the first sensible car analogy. A buyer who needs a service provider or project consultant might mention this need to a trusted person and this trusted person recommends somebody to that buyer.

The beauty of this is that the recommended business is firmly in position one for getting some work. If the recommendation is of the first type, i.e. they have heard of good results occurring for other people, the recommended business will more than likely be asked to at least submit a proposal. If the recommendation is of the second type, i.e. the trusted person has actually used the recommended business and had pleasing results, there is likely to be a much easier path to closing the deal for the recommended business in this situation.

Suppose that you knew a number of people who would be happy to recommend you because they trusted you. They either knew of your working reputation or, better still, had some pleasing work done for them by you. Wouldn't that be a boost for your business?

Well, this is what networking can do for you. The people you will meet at a networking event will usually have clients that they work with. They will hopefully be trusted by those clients. As long as your service offerings do not overlap with theirs and they trust you enough to recommend you; that is what they will do.

In case you were wondering, it is not all one way traffic.

People like to help others and they also like to be useful. If they recommend a good person to one of their clients then their own status goes up in the eyes of that client.

You will also be looking to, and expected to, recommend them to your own clients when the opportunity presents itself and therefore be in the position of helping both them and your own client.

The above referral scenarios represent hugely desirable outcomes for all concerned. When everything goes to plan that's the potentially powerful result of networking.

A bit of perspective

Although networking can sound like the cure for all your business marketing ills, let's take a minute or two to think about it carefully.

Networking, when approached and executed well, is a marvellous marketing tool for any business. Be aware, however, that it is just that; a marketing tool. Moreover, it is merely one marketing tool among many marketing tools available to you.

I would personally strongly caution you against relying solely on referral marketing as your source of leads. Why do I say this?

I am sure that there are many people out there doing extremely well relying on networking referrals alone and you may be able to cite numerous examples yourself. My point is that your business is your business and as such is unique. In my experience, there is never a one size fits all method for anything, especially in business sales and marketing. There may be many other approaches out there that will yield you equal or better results with less investment of time and money. It would be unwise of you not to explore or at least consider alternatives.

I would recommend that you seek out businesses that are similar to yours and investigate the ways that they market themselves. If you get to know them, you could quiz them as to what works best or what works poorly. I am not saying that you have to copy all, or even any, of their tactics but I would recommend you at least check out other methods of getting to market that might be beneficial to you. Be aware also that tactics that work well for other businesses may work poorly for you and vice versa.

Consider talking to a business marketing advisor, one hopefully recommended to you by a trusted friend, who is experienced in helping businesses similar to yours. You should come up with a balanced strategy for marketing that suits both you and your business.

Once you begin to network at the organised events you may find it is quite addictive. You will meet a large number of pleasant people and talk about many interesting things. It is easy to spend a lot of money and time that may have been better spent on client projects. I have provided much more detail on monitoring returns in Chapter 8.

I cannot stress enough the importance of doing your research before committing to any expenditure relating to networking. You have to make careful study of the myriad of options out there. Use your existing network for this and speak to people that you trust. You will always make some mistakes as this is inevitable in business and life. With a bit of research and thought you should keep them to a minimum. I will highlight problem areas as we go along. I have made many mistakes (some basic general ones and some probably unique to me) and will endeavour to keep you on the straight and narrow as you prepare for business networking success.

Networking aims and strategy

As we have discussed, the overall aim of the business networking process is to create and maintain high quality relationships with other business people. These high quality relationships will lead to referrals and positive advocacy for you. This outcome will serve to grow your reputation, your business and your profits and of course you will be doing all this for others as well.

This is the ideal situation to aim at. Getting there is not always easy of course; it takes patience and time.

Remember that this book is about your journey to successful business networking. It is not a book about sales or selling. Selling has its own myriad and varied array of strategies and models; all describing what works best. Do not confuse networking and selling. Learn to do each well and you will prosper.

You will likely read, or will already have read, a lot of literature, adverts and even some books by people who will tell you that they have the ultimate short-cut solution to networking and how they will teach you to guarantee huge sales each and every time you visit a venue. They will always promise to give you the secret sales tools that no-one can resist for a price. The best way for them to make money is to sell secret tools to people and they do it well. I personally stay clear of these people and their guaranteed systems. If you find one that works and you can live with it then I wish you well.

The style of business networking that I discuss in this book is a proven marketing tool that should prove to be a valuable addition to your marketing toolkit and strategy.

Learn your ABC's

I will be talking throughout this book about the strategy that I use personally and which will serve you well as you begin your business networking journey. It has served me well because it works. It is a repeatable process that closely follows the natural way humans interact and become friends. I have framed it in the easily remembered form of Levels A, B & C because getting the fundamentals right is the key to success in any endeavour and we all started out with learning our ABC's. It is for information only of course – never mention to anyone that they are at a certain level in your contact hierarchy. It is only useful to help you navigate the world of networking.

The key to networking is to be memorable in a good way. If people remember you favourably they will use your skills or refer your skills to others.

Here is a brief overview of the three levels.

Level A is associated with acquaintance. It is the stage where people first get to meet you, find out who you are and understand a little bit about what you can do for them. You in turn get to know them and what they can do for you. This level will form the bulk of your connections and most people will remain at this level because you will simply be unable to, or want to, form deeper relationships with them.

Level B is associated with belief. It is the stage where people believe in what you do as a business professional and they see, hear, understand and believe in the business benefits that you have to offer them or others. At this level people might also ask for advice and they might refer you on to others or at least introduce you as a known quantity.

Level C is the stage you definitely want to be at. It is associated with confidence, collaboration and co-operation. People will happily have you work for them, they will work with you, they will refer you and they may even act as your advocate by introducing you directly to their own clients. You should be doing the same for them of course.

From now on I will use the terms Level A, Level B and Level C for written clarity.

Remember that Level C is the desired business networking relationship level that you should be aiming at.

Bear in mind that the ABC strategy is a continuous process. You will have to be actively engaged in all stages during your business networking activity.

Level A Connections

You will make many acquaintances at this level. Awareness and appreciation are the first two components that need to be established as you are aiming to build a network of people who know about you and know something about your business. You also need to know about others and something about their businesses. This is the most basic level of your networking connection hierarchy. It will also be far and away the largest level because you will know of and know something about quite a few people and businesses although you won't yet be friendly with them, believe in them, co-operate with them or have confidence in them.

There are numerous ways of becoming known to and appreciated by other people and businesses but in this book we will be focusing purely on interacting with people in face to face situations. There are also numerous places to start the process. I go into much more detail about this in Chapter 2.

Awareness simply means that other people are aware that you actually exist. You are also now aware that they exist as business entities at this basic level.

Appreciation simply means that other people know what you do and, more importantly, what you can do for them. You will know the same about them too.

Your method and style of networking introduction is the key to making this stage of the process successful and you will read a much more about this vital stage of the process in Chapter 4.

People will want to meet and uncover the real you, so be prepared to reveal your real personality over time. Don't wear your heart on your sleeve from minute one but generally be as transparent and honest as possible and also be willing to share appropriate bits of your personal life if required. You should expect the same honesty back of course.

We cannot all be the life and soul of the party or be able to share our innermost feelings; in reality no-one expects us to do this. We are all different people with varying degrees of extroversion and introversion in our personalities. As a simplistic definition, introverts are generally reflective people who process information internally before vocalising their thoughts or feelings and extroverts are generally outgoing people who like to openly discuss their thoughts and ideas with others and freely share their feelings. Networking can often be something of an ordeal for introverts. Extroverts can see them as too quiet or non-assertive. Conversely, extroverts can thrive in the face to face environment of networking yet can sometimes be seen as aggressive and pushy by introverts. Throughout the book I will offer thoughts, strategies and techniques that will help everyone to work together and gain benefits.

You should always be consistent in your networking activities. By making a real effort to keep in some sort of contact with the majority of Level A members in your network, they will see or speak to you that much more and therefore get to be aware of you and appreciate your offerings that much more. You will be on their collective radar so to speak. You will of course get to be aware and appreciate them so much more as well.

You will now begin, hopefully, to move some of your Level A connections on to the next stage of the process which is of course Level B.

Level B Connections

Your connections at Level B will now believe in you. They will believe that you are a serious, competent and consistent business person with a good, credible business message and offering. You should, of course, live up to that belief and be professional and consistent in your approach at all times. They may well befriend you and you may also befriend them at this level. Connections that you consider are believable will also be at this level in your contact hierarchy.

Business people who believe in you and your expertise would readily consider asking for your advice or input and might even consider referring you to others at this stage if a suitable opportunity arose.

Keep bearing in mind that you are always aiming for quality business relationships. You will not be befriended or even liked by all the business people you meet and, in turn, you will not befriend or like all of them either. It is completely unrealistic to think otherwise and if you try and be all things to all people nobody will ever get to the real you. You might even lose sight of the real you in the process.

Also be aware that the numbers in your business network circle at each level of the ABC process should reduce. Therefore, there should be substantially less people at Level B than at Level A in your list of contacts. It is simply a factor of the time available to spend on maintaining each of your business relationships and the depth of those various business relationships. Everyone's time, especially yours, is highly valuable nowadays and must be maximised.

You have to go for quality over quantity if all parties in the deeper level relationships are to benefit.

Level C Connections

The real business networking benefits start at the Level C stage of the ABC process. Level C is where you should aim for as a networker.

At Level C, people will have a lot of confidence in you and will genuinely and willingly want to work with you or have you do work for them. They will co-operate with you on joint projects and proposals. They will happily and proactively recommend you to others if asked or if an appropriate opportunity presents itself.

They may even become positive advocates for you; actively and enthusiastically looking for opportunities for you, as they work with their own clients and customers.

You should be acting the same way on their behalf as well and you will find that a system of mutual support can develop. Help will be offered without an instant reciprocation being required. Remember, what goes around comes around in the world of business and business networking, as with so much of life.

You should aim to have a small group of people, that you have full confidence in, at the core of your business network. You should also aim to be in the core Level C group of as many of your network contacts as possible. This will maximise your potential to be referred.

Over time, you will probably form close bonds with your trusted core and you will likely become good friends. Being your own boss can be a lonely activity sometimes and it is an added bonus to have a group of people you can use as a sounding board for ideas, advice and sometimes to have a good rant.

You will have to earn this Level C status over time and then work hard to maintain it. Consistently deliver on all your promises, give help, information and referrals and continue to demonstrate that you're a credible, competent and professional business person with integrity and honesty who can show measurable and visible results.

All of the above takes patience, time and hard work. I never said or claimed it would be easy. There are no quick fixes or shortcuts here.

What you do not want to do when networking

Business networking is, or should be, all about building relationships.

What you must never do is directly try and sell to anyone when networking. This is the most annoying thing you can do in a networking situation. I have been on the receiving end of this many times and I now take steps to avoid those people whenever I see them. If you ignore the clear warning signs from people who don't want to be directly sold to, you will definitely be memorable but for all the wrong reasons.

So don't simply hand out your cards and brochures to anyone who comes within range then start telling them why they should buy from you, call you or book an appointment with you.

Now, it is perfectly possible that someone you meet is keen to work with you or buy from you right from the start; marvellous news. Be aware that this has now become a straight selling situation.

If you are at an event of some kind, do not attempt to start negotiation or planning the sale straight away. Make arrangements to talk with them more after the event is over. You can then arrange a meeting or even take an order in comfort without embarrassing the potential customer or annoying anyone else there.

Be memorable for all the right reasons by following the ABC strategy.

Chapter 2 - Where to network best and with whom

Where can you network successfully?

The accurate but not overly helpful answer is that you can network successfully almost anywhere where you can meet and talk to other people.

It all depends on your confidence and ability to communicate and network well but it is hugely important to always be ready and willing to tell people about the benefits that you can offer them or others. You are a business marketer after all so you need to feel comfortable, confident and authentic when promoting yourself out there in the world. There will be much more about this aspect of networking in Chapter 4.

You can in fact network with almost any individual you meet. They may not be in business themselves but they will often be associated with or related to people who are.

In a purely social situation, you would have to do weigh up the pros and cons. If someone asks you what you do then tell them but do it in a conversational and brief way and only go further if they express more interest. If they don't show anything other than polite interest then drop it and enjoy your day. Don't lose potential friends by being pushy or they will definitely remember you for all the wrong reasons.

Random interactions with other business people at any time are always worth a brief conversation and potential exchange of details. I am thinking of trains, planes, hotel foyers, waiting rooms, etc...

If you are visiting any business as a customer and you feel that your services may be of interest then by all means approach the manager or owner for a brief chat and a summary of what you can potentially do for them. Offer to follow up later in some way if they are receptive. Play it low key and who knows what could develop. Remember that they will know other business people too.

General business events such as award ceremonies, seminars, dinners, exhibitions, conferences, training workshops, etc... can be perfect for networking. These events can be free or paid for. In most cases they are not specifically structured for networking but will have networking time built in to the programs. It will be up to you to network without becoming a nuisance – a label not good for you or your business. By the way, I define a nuisance networker as someone who simply shows up at any old event and gets right to directly selling whatever it is they have to offer to anyone they can latch onto. Please do not do this. When approached correctly, with a view to establishing initial contact with follow-up later, there is nothing wrong with doing your networking at these business events and I would heartily recommend attending as many as possible to see how you get on.

Many business people neglect to network with existing clients. That's right. The easiest people to sell to are people who are already your customers. Likewise, the best referrals are often internal between one department or division head and another. Don't forget this valuable resource. When you are with a good client and the opportunity presents itself, talk with other people there about their issues and how you can possibly help.

The final place to network is the one that most people associate with the term business networking; the organised business networking group events.

This book is aimed at helping you understand and do well at these types of networking events. These events are generally run by for-profit organisations or networking companies. The format and structure of these organisations and events varies enormously as does the cost. The contact suitability for your requirements will vary enormously as well. I will analyse all three of these main factors as well as some minor ones and help you make sense of the options to choose a suitable group. I am assuming this is a likely way for you to want to proceed because you are reading this book.

How to choose an organised networking group

Nowadays there are many types of organised business networking groups and events available. Initially, it is difficult to decide which ones to join or go to.

You simply can't go to all of them so you will need some sort of selection process and selection criteria.

One aspect you should look at is cost.

There are some networking groups out there that don't charge a joining fee or event admission fee. They do not provide much in the way of refreshments or structure so are more of a social event where you do your own networking. The quality of businesses attending can be variable and you have to be confident in your own abilities when you network there. I wouldn't rule them out though. Like everything else, try it and make up your own mind.

You will almost certainly have to pay a fee to join most organised networking groups and there will often be a per-event charge on top of this. For your money you should expect well hosted events, a networking friendly structure, refreshments and a pleasant location.

The fees are also highly variable and do not always reflect the quality of the group or events. Do your research and ask your friends and business colleagues which ones they attend or can recommend. Don't sign up to the first one you attend even if it seems to fit the bill. Your time and money is valuable and you need to spend it in a smart manner. Take every opportunity to use any free trials or guest invitations the networking groups may offer before you commit. Hosts and salespeople can be persuasive when trying to get new clients on board. Be sure to confirm any claims they make and check out their list of current members. Phone a few people at random, not the ones the host recommends, and have a quick chat. Most people are happy to provide feedback

Another aspect you could look at is event structure.

Some networking group events are run in a highly structured manner with little deviation to the program agendas. Some also have mandatory weekly attendance and weekly member referral requirements. Some groups are so laid back and informal and you have to work hard to avoid them being merely social events. The middle ground format should have reasonable structure to ensure quality networking takes place but also some flexibility to allow a bit of program variation on the day. Some even offer expert speaker slots from within the membership and these can be interesting and provide some good exposure for the businesses that do it. I talk more on the benefits of this in Chapter 9. Of course everyone has their own preference so, once again, try them all out before you sign up. Ask any of your friends and business colleagues who already attend these type of events which meeting structures they prefer and why.

The final main aspect you should consider is your target or ideal client. I personally think this is the most important of the three main criteria.

It makes no sense to attend networking group events when your ideal clients, or links to your ideal clients, are absent. As mentioned previously most of the networking groups are organised as for-profit businesses and as a result they are keen to attract new paying members. If you consider the fact that most people who join these groups are new businesses looking for clients in much the same way you are, the odds are against you directly meeting an actual economic buyer of your service or product. Depending on the level of businesses that the networking group targets the member businesses may not be able to refer you to your ideal clients either.

In a well-chosen and appropriate networking group, good solid referrals frequently happen. In an inappropriate group for your business needs, good referrals are rare. People are generally busy working hard for their own business development and are not necessarily acting with high integrity or with respect for others.

Your ideal clients are simply the people or organisations that will benefit from your offering and will be willing and able to pay your price for that benefit. What businesses might they run? What level will they be at? What issues or improvements might they need? What finances do they have available? Where are they located geographically? Where do they network? The list goes on.

I recommend spending a lot of time and effort to identify your ideal client. Go as far as you can in producing both a male and a female version. Name them and give ages, hobbies and as much biographical information to them as possible. You should know and understand your ideal client as well as any member of your family or your best friend; in terms of business they should become your best and most profitable friend. You will address your networking message to them all the time. People who aren't your ideal clients will still recognise them and hopefully refer you to them if you are memorable enough.

If all this sounds like a description of targeted marketing to you then you are quite correct. Make no mistake, no matter what main business you may think you are in, clearly remember that you are also solidly in the marketing business.

How do you target these ideal clients in the networking context? The answer is simply to network where they do. For example, if you are targeting CEO's of larger companies for your leadership coaching offerings then you need to know where these CEO's go to network. They might go to business dinners, director level networking groups, industry conventions, business seminars and talks, award ceremonies, etc... The key for you is to go there as well.

Match your networking techniques to your chosen arena. The events will likely be social in nature so treat them as such. You have to be confident that you are at peer level with them and appear to be fully at home in the environment. Low key introductions are often sufficient to announce your presence. If they like what you do they will approach you but this takes time, patience, confidence, integrity, belief and financial investment.

Of course, you have to profoundly understand what your business actually offers before you can design an ideal client and then seek them out. What do you do and more importantly what do you do that is beneficial to the client? You need to be crystal clear on this because if you are unclear then everybody else, a group which includes your ideal clients, will be unclear as well.

Some networking formats will better suit trade based businesses rather than consultancy providers and may not have the depth of referral coverage you seek or need. Each brand of networking group organisation is different. Each group has different types of businesses as members. Each host has different styles, contacts and skills. Be sure and check out their list of current members before signing. I have seen a group that stated they only had top economic decision makers and directors as members and it was by invitation only. When I had a look at their member list this was patently not the case; caveat emptor or buyer beware.

Other factors such as the time or dates that the groups meet as well as their geographic location may also have a bearing on which group you ultimately choose to join.

You may need to travel a bit or pay more money to join a group that is absolutely right for your business but remember that one solid referral to an ideal client will more than cover this and move your business right along the path you planned. The payback potential for you is much higher in these ideal environments and you can build solid business relationships at this level in a much more sustainable way. Saving yourself a few pounds to attend a local and cheap series of events with low level business members may be a frustrating waste of your valuable time and money.

Take the time to choose the right networking group, member profile and event format for both you and your business. It is important that you get it as accurate for your needs as possible from the start. You may even decide that two or more groups will better suit your needs.

It takes commitment, time and focus to gain the most benefit from networking. Make sure you are with people and businesses that you truly want to spend this time and effort with.

Chapter 3 - Your networking mind-set

Your networking mind-set is a vital and sometimes overlooked part of the whole networking experience. In fact, your mind-set is a vital part of your whole business experience. Life is always made easier with a positive and effective attitude.

The way your body functions and performs at any given moment in your life is given the general term physiology. For our purposes, and with regard to networking, talking about your physiology refers mainly to how you stand, look, project emotion, move and feel. There are many more but these attributes will suffice to help you understand the importance of a good mind-set.

An interesting situation arises in that your state of mind can readily influence your physiology and vice versa.

If you play sport, music or undertake any other form of skilled activity, you will be well aware that a positive mind-set affects the way you play and perform. When you are in the perfect mind-set for the activity things happen almost effortlessly and it almost all goes to plan; you could be said to be in the zone. Even when there is a set-back, you take it in your stride with good grace and simply move on.

Conversely, you will also no doubt be familiar with the outcome when you are not in the right mind-set for the task or activity. Almost anything that you attempt seems to take huge effort and everything you touch seems to be of poor quality. When there is a set-back, however slight, it appears to be a mighty disaster and you react wholly out of proportion. Things often go from bad to worse.

It is the same when you are interacting with other people. If you have a positive and useful state of mind, it follows that you will have a positive and useful physiology. If this positive physiology then projects to the world and you get positive feedback this enhances your positive mind-set still further. It is now a virtuous circle; you feel good and your physiology gets ever more positive and useful.

If, however, you have a negative and non-useful state of mind, it follows that you will have a negative and non-useful physiology. If this negative physiology then projects to the world you may well get negative feedback. This then reinforces your negative mind-set and can become a vicious circle; making you feel worse and your physiology yet more negative.

If you are in a good mind-set for networking you will likely present your best features to the world and give yourself the best chance of a positive outcome to the networking experience.

This positive mind-set and associated useful physiology idea applies whether you are networking socially one on one, at a formal business event or you are at an organised business networking group.

It's all too easy for me to talk about a positive and useful networking mind-set but what do I actually mean by it and how do you go about achieving it?

Here are three essentials for successful networking:

A spirit of curiosity

A spirit and attitude of genuine curiosity will ensure that you show an interest in others and therefore be open to opportunities as they present themselves. You will also become more interesting to them. People like people who pay them favourable attention.

When you are curious you can also use your physiology to demonstrate this to others. Lean in towards them slightly and listen attentively. Frequent nodding in agreement and the use of appropriate encouraging words will keep the other people talking. When other people talk and you listen you will almost always gain valuable information.

A relaxed state of mind

A relaxed state of mind will allow you to take most things in your stride and create a relaxed state in others.

Use whatever techniques work best for you, but ensure that you relax before you network. First impressions are formed quickly as I will discuss in Chapter 6. Make sure you help create those good first impressions by being as relaxed as possible.

Being relaxed allows you to think, look and behave at your best. You will have time to think and respond. You will appear highly confident and professional. You will have the best chance of getting your message across and being favourably remembered.

Your physiology, language and bearing will transmit to others and they will relax too. If you exhibit poor physiology or appear nervous and flustered at events, this can be off-putting to other people and they will likely focus on those negatives rather than your positive message. You will be remembered for the wrong reasons.

An attitude of patience

An attitude of patience is a must as you will initially be sowing and nurturing seeds that may take some time to grow and ripen.

Never seek instant returns from networking interactions. If you help someone or refer them on, don't expect instant reciprocation. It could happen straight away of course but don't count on it. Enjoy the simple fact that you have been of help to someone you met and move on to the next interaction. The repayment for your help may come along much later and from a wholly unexpected or unknown source. For example, that person may have mentioned you to a client and they approach you directly.

Networking and the building of business relationships takes time and a long-term focus.

Good things come to those who are patient but not necessarily to those that simply wait and take no action.

Before any networking opportunity, be it one on one or in a group, try this simple exercise which will help to relax you and put you in a useful networking mind-set.

Stand up straight and take a few deep breaths then repeat this affirmative mantra quietly to yourself, several times, immediately prior to the start of any networking activity.

"I am curious, I am relaxed and I am patient"

Trust me, it works wonders.

If you want to work at a deeper level with controlling all your mental and emotional states you can practice the following simple exercise whenever you have some spare time and some peace and quiet. You have nothing to lose by trying this technique and quite a lot to gain.

Get relaxed and comfortable in the way that suits you best at the time. If you are familiar and comfortable with any breath related relaxation techniques feel free to use them. When you are relaxed, ask yourself the following questions and take the time to fully reflect on your answers.

Recall a time you were in a poor emotional or mental state and what triggered it? How did your body feel? What thoughts were in your mind? How did others react to you? How useful was this state for you and others?

Recall a time when you were in a fantastic emotional or mental state? How did your body feel? What thoughts were in your mind? How did others react to you? How useful was this state for you and others?

What was the difference between the two scenarios? How could you use knowledge of this difference to help yourself switch to the more useful state?

Try to use different scenarios each time to build up a picture of your states and possible ways you can move from one to the other.

For example, suppose you were in a frustrated state of mind because of something that had gone wrong earlier in the day. Simply recognising that you are in such a non-useful state is an excellent starting point. What state would now serve you best? Would you be better served by an optimistic state of mind perhaps? Well, you could recall your exact physiology when you were last in an optimistic state and simply reproduce it. This will automatically be more useful to you and you will also begin to think more optimistically as well. Before too long you will have changed your state to one of useful optimism.

Practice this exercise as often as you can and in time you may find you can change your emotional and mental state almost at will. It is an incredibly useful skill for you to develop.

One last observation regarding your mind-set is to try at all times in your life to surround yourself with positive people and positive experiences. Negative people are a terrible drain on your spirits so try and limit your exposure to them. Examine your relationships with certain people and how you feel after interacting with them. How do you think people feel after interacting with you? It is an interesting exercise and can be very illuminating. Like attracts like so make sure you are positive and positive people will naturally gravitate towards you.

Chapter 4 - Get your networking message right

What is your real aim as a networker?

Your aim as a networker is to find people or organisations that either are your ideal clients or who know those ideal clients and will refer you on to them.

Once you have found those people or organisations you need to inform them of your business and what you can do for them or the people they know.

You have to be memorable to those people, in a highly positive way, so that they will have confidence in you and use your skills when they have need or refer you to others when the opportunity arises.

To be memorable you must be able to both cut through the noise of the modern world with your message and also make that message sticky enough to leave a lasting impression on them. I use the term sticky to refer to a message, or part of a message, that literally sticks in the other person's brain for some reasonable and useful length of time. This is the goal of all advertisers and marketers. Remember that you are a marketer of your business no matter what else you think you do.

I have discussed the ABC strategy and how you connect with people on all the three levels to form a solid business referral relationship with someone. I have also discussed where you can best network, how you can start to identify your ideal clients and also given some guidance on where to look for your ideal clients.

I will now talk about how you can start to cut through the noise and leave that sticky message; creating a memorable impression of yourself and your business offering.

I am going to spend a lot of time on this aspect of your networking skills because I believe it to be the most important of all. It is no use getting in front of the right people and giving a great first impression and then simply not delivering an impactful and highly memorable message about yourself and your business. It all flows from the solid foundation you create when you can fully understand your business offering, the beneficial results it offers to your ideal client and how to memorably and successfully transmit that message to them.

You need an effective and dynamic introduction

What you say and how you say it is extremely important in all communications but especially so when networking. I've already stated that you should never sell products or services directly but you do have to sell yourself and your business offerings. You have to do it in a way that satisfies the ABC strategy, maintains your dignity and is sticky enough to leave a good and memorable impression with the other person.

In my experience, most people new to networking make the same basic mistake when starting out. I certainly made this mistake and I quickly worked out why I was not successful in getting referrals or even any favourable attention.

When asked by someone else in a networking situation, "What is your business all about?" or something similar, most people state their job title and business name then simply present a list of the things that they offer and the things that they do. They often don't pay much, or even any, attention to the other person or their needs. If the other person is doing the same thing then the whole interaction is essentially pointless. You might as well have stayed at the office or at home.

You may have heard of something called the elevator pitch. If not, the term comes from the early days of sales and marketing and it refers to a short script that could be recited at short notice to pitch a product or service and generate favourable interest i.e. the busy CEO gave the sales rep the time it took the elevator or lift to get to the top floor – hence the elevator pitch.

You may have heard this term being used in networking circles and even been advised to get or develop such an elevator pitch for yourself.

I think there is much confusion caused by the use of this term in relation to networking.

You are not actually there to pitch at all. Pitching is a sales term and you should not be aiming to sell directly in any networking environment. You should simply be introducing yourself and your business in order to make acquaintances, build credibility, referrals and create trust. Always think this way in terms of your introduction.

Creating a favourable first impression is incredibly important in networking situations. You can make a fantastic first impression with both your verbal communication and your non-verbal communication. You can also make an extremely poor first impression and these are often hard to come back from. I will have more to say about your non-verbal communication skills in Chapter 6.

For now we will discuss and deal only with your verbal networking message which is aimed at your ideal client.

You definitely need a brief, effective, well-crafted and dynamic introduction, to both yourself and your business, to try and connect quickly and favourably with the people you meet when networking. Once you have connected like this you can then decide whether or not to take the contact further along in the process of your ABC strategy.

Some of the many beneficial results of a carefully crafted and effective networking introduction are:

You will create a clear impression of what you can do for the other person or for the people that they may be connected to.

You will leave them with something highly memorable that will enable them to reconnect with you easily at subsequent meetings.

You will leave them with something memorable that will enable them to easily recall both you and your services. This makes it more likely that they will call on you or refer you in the future.

You will filter out or pre-qualify people who will never be clients or will be unlikely or unable to refer you or your services to others. They may simply be competitors. Valuable time is saved by all parties and this allows you all to carry on networking and thus maximise your time.

You will quickly filter out people you don't like and people who don't like you. This may sound harsh but it is a fact of life; get over it and move on with a smile.

Notice that I used the word dynamic in relation to your introduction. Dynamic refers to the fact that is will constantly change to suit the circumstances. It is of no benefit for you to constantly use one scripted introduction for everyone you meet. We will fully examine how to be flexible and fully present in the moment so that your introduction and style will remain fresh for you and your potential connections.

Before we look at constructing the memorable and sticky message proper, let's look at a couple of things from the sales world that will have a strong bearing on the way you craft your message.

"What's in it for me?" and "Promote beneficial results not features."

The "What's in it for me?" factor

The common phrase "What's in it for me?" is generally abbreviated to WIIFM (pronounced *whiff-um*) and I shall adopt the same shorthand from this point onwards.

Humans are basically time-selfish creatures. We are wired up that way from our earliest evolutionary ancestors onward. Back then we needed time to hunt for food, mate, make tools or sleep. Anything that distracted us and enticed us to spend time away from our main pursuits had to be worth the cost. In modern times our time and attention is becoming more and more valuable and rare every day; when we give up some of it we want maximum value for that time and attention.

You don't believe me? You have given up time to read this book. You are doing it to get some valuable insights into modern business networking. I have to provide the value and results you seek or you will put the book down and walk away. The WIIFM factor for you is "Am I learning something useful and gaining something valuable with my time and attention? Have I got my desired results?"

Fully understanding this fact is incredibly important. I have to satisfy your WIIFM factor so you will read, enjoy, learn and hopefully buy and read more of my work. I in turn would ultimately like to develop a business relationship with you, or someone you refer me too, at some future point; that is my WIIFM factor. Everyone is after something for their favourable time and attention nowadays. They want their WIIFM factor satisfied. Everybody's time is getting less and less available and becoming much more valuable.

So, how do you satisfy the WIIFM factor of the person stood in front of you in a networking situation?

You must promote beneficial results and not features.

Promote beneficial results not features

You are at networking events to promote yourself and your business. This is done in the same way that you should promote any product.

One of the golden rules is to promote beneficial results and not features. So, what does this mean in networking terms?

You have to satisfy WIIFM factor in your prospective client or referral partner by offering them something so compelling that they become hooked and want to be attentive to your message. They must feel that there is real value in what you offer; value to them or to people they may be connected with. You also have to do it quickly and effectively so their attention stays focused on you.

The following is an extremely simplistic description, or model, of how any conversation is achieved between two people.

One person, the sender, forms a message they would like to send, encodes this message into language then transmits this message, as well as they can, to the other person.

The other person, the receiver, hears the message, attempts to decode it and understand it then formulates a suitable response based on the new information.

The conversation proceeds back and forth until done.

I said it is a simplistic model because there are many factors that have a bearing on the outcome of each part, or transaction, between the participants. Each person has a rich personal and social history. Each person has a unique set of beliefs and values. Each person has a particular genetic make-up that predisposes certain attitudes and styles of communication and response. Each person has a unique level of linguistic skill and vocabulary.

Due to the vast amount of noise and data entering our communication systems, we also unconsciously delete information we don't deem important, we unconsciously generalise from specifics and we also unconsciously distort information to fit in with our view of the world.

Even assuming that the people speak the same language and at the same level of ability, it is amazing that we can be understood at all; even with ideal conditions.

How many times have you said something that seemed simple, innocuous and obvious in its meaning to you only to find that the other person completely missed the point, misinterpreted it and flew into a rage? Why did this happen? Who is actually at fault here? Is it the sender or the receiver? Can we do anything about this?

The basic reason is that words themselves have no meaning. It is the person hearing the words that applies meaning to them. Moreover, that person applies their particular meaning, based on their unique view and perception of the world. This is an important point to remember. Choose your words carefully and ensure that your meaning and message intent are fully understood before moving on in a conversation.

The responsibility for the success of any communication lies fairly and squarely on the shoulders of the sender. If you are the sender then it is your problem if the other person does not understand your message; alter your message until they do understand.

It is a sad fact that many people in the modern world have even forgotten that a conversation is actually a two-way dialogue. Many people also do not listen well and I will talk more fully about this at the end of Chapter 4. Suffice it to say that, when interacting with others, people generally need to be liked. They also want to be seen as clever and not making mistakes.

People tend to be thinking about what they are going to say next and will they sound good saying it. When this happens they pay no attention to the other person and the things that they are saying. This behaviour leads to two people talking at each other rather than to each other. No information passes between them at all and nothing useful is learned by either party.

Whilst it was only the briefest of descriptions of the vast field of communication, all of the above information helps to explain why there are so many poor quality interactions occurring in both our general, social and business lives.

Networking interactions are obviously not immune. In fact, they may be more prone to this single-sidedness effect due to the fact that people are trying hard to impress and promote themselves even more than usual. This leads to the reciting of job titles and laundry lists of activity that we are all becoming skilled at filtering out and ignoring. For example, any one accountant, lawyer or business consultant seems to be the same as every other nowadays. How do you differentiate yourself?

Clearly, your primary concern is to capture the other person's favourable interest and attention. The first step you should take with improving your message is to promote all your services and business offerings as beneficial results; beneficial results for the other person of course, not you.

Describing beneficial results for people is the best way to trigger their WIIFM detector. They will pay more attention when they think there is something to be gained; either for themselves or for their clients. This is human nature so use it to your advantage and don't fight it.

Converting features to beneficial results

When you list a service or feature of your business you risk being filtered out or simply ignored by the other person. If you do get their attention you are then relying completely on that person analysing your feature and deciding for themselves that it offers a beneficial result for them or others. This could happen but is more likely not to happen.

What is a beneficial result anyway? A beneficial result is anything that gives someone what they want or need. Gaining more profit, reducing costs, increasing productivity, more time at home, reducing maintenance costs, more time off, improving sales, better health, more security, etc…. are all examples of beneficial results. Beneficial results vary widely from person to person and business to business because everyone is unique.

Note that there are logical beneficial results such as the business or financial ones listed above and there are emotional beneficial results such as those involving free time, family and health. The emotional ones carry more weight and influence with people. If you can trigger these you will get the most attention and positive interest.

There are examples from the world of sales all around you. Examine advertisements to see how they target and promote logical and emotional benefits. How do those adverts hook you and catch your interest? Don't sell high grade concrete, sell a beautiful driveway. Don't sell paint, sell beautiful walls. Don't sell pots and pans, sell delicious meals. Promote the beneficial results to the other person that you and your business can provide for them.

If you can find out what the other person you are talking to values, logically and emotionally, as beneficial results then you are well on your way to providing those results and building a solid business relationship. Be assured, I will talk more about finding out this information using skilful questioning techniques in Chapter 6.

For now let us examine how to turn a feature or service into a beneficial result with an example that builds from a feature oriented message to a fully beneficial results oriented message. Note that all three messages are of similar length.

A feature oriented statement example could be:

"Our software quickly and efficiently streamlines your sales and prospecting status. We use a real-time state of the art, data-driven processing engine that links all your business processes seamlessly. It all integrates into a single dashboard so you can easily link your company intranet to your external financial and logistical hubs."

The above information might appeal to an IT Manager or service technician during a late-stage sales presentation. They might see many beneficial results that your offering has for them. However, in a networking scenario, it is unlikely to have an instant appeal to the majority of the people that you talk to. I was actually bored when writing this version and I certainly wouldn't want to hear it at an event. Even if the person you talk to uses sales software they will struggle to see any real advantages when the features are presented like this. You may be memorable but not for good reasons.

Let's try again and this time we'll add some benefits.

"Our sales software, Sales Pro Soft 2, takes up to twenty percent less time per sales transaction completion, on average, than any existing system. This could mean a saving of up to two hours during a normal day. We use the latest web-based cloud server technology that keeps your data integrity intact."

This is better. It offers people the benefits of time saving and also data safety. These could well be important to some of the people you meet. You may get some interest and attention. You have also named the actual product. Is it memorable? It wouldn't be of direct use to me but would I remember it for possible referral to people I might know? I still don't think so. The problem for me is that the beneficial results, although useful, are presented too logically. The whole message is too logical and technical. I would probably not retain this information much beyond the end of our immediate conversation because I was never fully hooked and there is nothing sticky or memorable. There is also no personal connection. The word *you* does not appear anywhere. This had not created any emotional connection between the message and the recipient; this is hard to capture and attention will be lost.

How about this final version?

"All our customers love the simplicity, speed, power and security of the Sales Pro Soft 2 automated sales system. You like your golf don't you Andy? Well just think, you could easily make all your sales targets and get to the golf club up to two hours earlier each and every working day."

This is a big improvement. It is same length as the previous two versions yet achieves so much more. You have the product name and now four logical beneficial results are included. You have also introduced a new dynamic in terms of saying that "All our customers love…" This is powerful technique that demonstrates peer acceptance and uptake of a product; a proven way to make others feel relaxed and more than justified with the potential purchase, recommendation or referral.

The real power of this statement is at the emotional level. You have established a connection with me by use of the word *you* and also addressing me by name. You have also included an emotional beneficial result of the golf time, hopefully after having pre-established that I like golf, and this would definitely get my attention. There is some cheeky humour with "… each and every working day." Humour when used well is a powerful tool for establishing and maintaining a connection.

The acquisition of your sales software is still of no interest to me personally, but your clever message and emotional content is sticky and memorable. Therefore, if I hear anyone else mention that they want new sales software, I will likely be thinking favourably of the golfing sales program and will likely mention you to them. This is the power of referral networking with a good well-crafted and effective message.

Listen carefully to what people are telling you and substitute in whatever activity or need they have that your service or product could provide beneficial results for, particularly on an emotional level.

What does your business actually do?

If you are struggling at this point to come up with a brief and effective business description for your introduction, you may need to take a much deeper and closer look at what business you are actually in.

Remember that if you struggle to clearly and briefly articulate your business and beneficial result offerings then who else will be able to understand it?

To use a tree based analogy, you may be looking at too many of the branches, twigs and leaves of your business rather than the whole tree. You are likely to be a highly detail oriented person and will naturally look at things in this detailed specific way.

Continuing with the tree analogy, you also may be looking at the whole forest and not actually seeing your particular business tree clearly. You are likely to be a big picture oriented person and will naturally look at things in this expansive way. It is advantageous to think big picture at this stage but as with so much in life it can be taken too far and made too general.

I will now illustrate a general thought process for building a dynamic and memorable networking message by way of two examples. One example will be about you running a product/service business and the other will be about you running a consultancy training business. There are many other business models of course but these two will suffice to demonstrate the general process. I will also build on and expand these examples over the next few sections, as different elements are brought in, to enhance them.

The following company messages are wholly fictitious and for illustration purposes only. I am aware of no such animal care company or sales training company. If you own similar businesses feel free to use the message elements as ready-made starting points for you. For everyone else simply adapt the various elements to suit your business goals, your experience and your personality.

Example one is about you running a business that sells animal care services and products. It has a wide range of potential clients given the fact that many people have pets, but you would like to form business connections with complementary organisations such as pet shops, veterinarians, kennels, stables, petting zoos, etc... The goal is to differentiate your business from all the other suppliers. You have a business that walks dogs, grooms pets and show animals, provides kennelling or stabling when owners are on holiday, supplies discount pet/animal feed, provides bedding material, provides animal training, offers animal nutrition advice and provides specialist handling and transport to and from the vets or a show, etc... You offer both products and services.

Example two is about a business that offers custom sales training, coaching and consultancy for other organisations that carry their own sales departments and sales teams. Target connections inside suitable client organisations would include CEO's, Organisational Development Officers, Sales Managers, Training Managers and possibly HR functions. You can provide customised sales presentation training for internal and external sales staff, you can analyse and improve sales operation work flows, you offer training options and scripting services for telesales staff, you install and implement various third party sales productivity tools such as customer relationship management (CRM) packages, you can offer customised sales induction, customer service and product training, you also work with sales manager development and you can also offer consultancy on client's own in-house training program effectiveness, etc... You offer mainly training services and consultancy with some third party product provision.

There are a lot of feature details in both these examples and, whilst they may well all be valuable links in your business chain, all these details can become extremely confusing for someone listening. Even if you turn all these into beneficial results it is still a long list. Your message in this form would put most people into a trance or confuse them entirely; you have now lost the chance to make an impression and gain that favourable attention to leave the sticky memory you need to succeed.

You also cannot rely on the recipient of your message being able or willing to make the connections necessary to understand the beneficial results of what you do from a list of your activities and services. You therefore have to control things yourself and present them with the connections in a memorable fashion.

An organised business networking group setting might allow you the time to get through it all but can you imagine someone in a social setting innocently asking you "What do you do?" then being hit with either of the lists given above. They would probably run away from you.

So, how can you come up with a much more brief and effective description, including the many beneficial results for them, of what you do?

The best way is to take a wider view of all the points above and try and find a common connection. This will not be easy for you detail people so ask yourself this question, "If I had to state what my business does in one reasonably short sentence, what would that sentence be?" Now ask, "Can I add at least one emotional beneficial result for a potential client."

Take your time as the answers are important to you.

I would say at this point that, if you are still having problems, you may want to ask a big picture style friend or colleague to help you. Doing this exercise will help you clarify your business model. You may need to rethink your whole business model if you are still struggling to simplify and state your core business premise or client benefits.

Here are two reasonable first versions, based on our fictitious companies, which we can examine:

"LuxPets is a one stop shop for all your pet or larger animal needs allowing you to focus on simply loving and enjoying your faithful friend while everything else is taken care of."

"Mighty Dynamite Sales Training can take over all your training and process design activity, allowing you and your key people to fully concentrate on their vital marketing and leadership functions, which will in turn keep you moving forward as a thriving business."

The LuxPets one is brief and highly *you* focused to get that vital personal connection. People with pets genuinely do love them so giving them more time to do that is a definite emotional benefit. Note that being a "one stop shop" is also a benefit but this time it is a logical one. The statement is big picture but gives enough information to prompt follow-up questions and engage interest. If you were talking to a pet owner they would likely be interested with it as is. If you were talking to a potential complementary business partner you may have to elaborate depending on their circumstances.

The Mighty Dynamite one is a bit longer but adequate for our needs. It is also highly *you* focused to get that all-important personal connection. Talking about freeing up time from the churn or mundane activities of training and process design is a definite emotional beneficial result for the busy executive. Using the term "thriving business" is also emotive as we are all out for a profit to help us survive and prosper. Note that using the term "activity" as the downside and "leadership functions" as an upside benefit, says a lot in relatively few words. Let the words you use do the heavy lifting in your message. Think quality not quantity and edit ruthlessly. The description is big picture but gives plenty of information to prompt follow-up questions and engage potential client interest. Any busy executive should be interested in hearing more about the potential for cost effective outsourcing.

We will work on making both of these more memorable and sticky but it is a workable start.

You can of course be too big picture and simply describing your business as *"I run a pet care business called LuxPets"* or *"Mighty*

Dynamite offers sales training and sales process design" is accurate but far too brief and impersonal. It may not capture any of that key initial interest you need; even from pet owners or sales managers.

Let us move on to triggering more of an emotional connection with our listeners and potential clients or referral partners.

What gets you up in the morning?

Let me ask you a question. Are you genuinely passionate about your business? Do you get up every day feeling totally enthusiastic about what it is that you actually do?

To be brutally honest with you, if you cannot answer an immediate and emphatic yes to those two questions, then you may have a bigger problem than simply how to succeed at networking. If you are in business solely for the money and are not truly passionate about the whole thing then you may have a hard time trying to persuade other people to get emotionally engaged with both you and your enterprise.

If you don't genuinely like your own business and you truly cannot get passionate or enthusiastic about it, then why should I or anyone else care one bit about it? Why should potential clients and referral partners care about your business? If no one cares about it then no-one will refer you.

Be aware that emotions and moods are highly infectious.

Enthusiasm is an extremely infectious emotion. Others will respond to that enthusiasm favourably. Even if they don't want your service or product themselves, they will almost certainly remember and like you; this should lead to good referrals for you. Exhibiting passion for what you do is also a memorable attitude.

Enthusiasm and passion show that you care about what you do and what you offer. Your physiology will also reflect your mood and emotion. You will be memorable and remembered for all the right reasons.

Apathy and disinterest are also infectious. You certainly don't want to pass these emotions on to people when networking. People will readily pick up on your mood of apparent boredom. Your whole body will scream out to them that you are only going through the motions. They will be bored and apathetic and pay you no favourable attention or remember you as anything other than a passing acquaintance. You might benefit from revisiting the section on mind-set and work on yours prior to any networking activity.

Ask yourself the question "What gets me out of bed in the morning?" Do you like your answer? I hope so.

When you have your honest answer, why not include it in your introduction?

We could add a bit to our *LuxPets* introduction:

"I love animals of all kinds and I love people who love animals. I think I might just have the best job in the world. LuxPets is the one stop shop for all your pet or larger animal needs. You can focus on simply loving and enjoying your faithful friend while everything else is taken care of for you."

We could also add a little bit to our *Mighty Dynamite* introduction but care must be taken not to sound too artificial with this type of intangible sale:

"Our fantastic service benefits essentially sell themselves and I'm the lucky one who gets to make people happy they discovered them. Mighty Dynamite Sales Training can take over all your training and process design activity, allowing you and your key people to fully concentrate on their vital marketing and leadership functions, which will in turn keep you moving forward as a thriving profitable business."

A short additional sentence, like the above examples, when it is added to your introduction, can punch way above its weight. It establishes your passion and enthusiasm as well as why you do this work in the first place and it does it straight away.

Because your words will neatly and clearly sum up what gets you out of bed in the morning, your physiology will back up your enthusiasm. People will get the fact that you are authentic and you will get instant credibility. You have started to create an attention grabbing message for your business.

Ask intriguing *you* questions

When anyone at a networking event asks me what I do or I have to do a brief introductory presentation I generally say something along the following lines:

"Have you ever heard a leader give a speech so dynamic and motivating that you wanted to jump up and get right to it? Have you ever heard a captivating presentation that simply flew by way too fast? Have you ever listened to a sales presentation and thought that you'd buy what they're selling whatever the price?

How about the flip-side?

Have you ever heard a leader you wouldn't follow to the fire exit in a fire even if it was the only one? Have you ever sat in a presentation and wished the projector would explode and end it all? Ever heard a sales presentation that was so bad they couldn't even give you their product for free?

It's a noisy old world nowadays. Communication skills are vital and you need people to want to listen to you and to fully understand your message.

I help business people to fully engage with their audiences and prospects. Working with me means that you'll get presentation skills, tools and techniques that can help you generate more leads, prospects and sales in an hour than most small businesses can generate in a month using other methods.

Tell me, how do you currently use your business building presentations?"

The whole sequence is highly *you* focused. I tailor it of course, depending on the situation and responses, but it gets people involved, thinking and engaged straight away. It is part story and part introduction and it gets them questioning exactly where they are in terms of their presentation skills or need. I use the appropriate delivery techniques to create maximum audience engagement and it demonstrates to them the power of speaking without ever mentioning a single feature.

They cannot help but grade their own speaking efforts based on my example extremes and they are almost always interested in knowing more. Many have not considered speaking skills as being so vital and they are intrigued. They also almost always mention someone else who needs to improve or an organisation that would benefit even if they don't. It pre-filters potential clients and referral partners and I also use the term "Working with me..." which puts the seed of that into their mind. I have found that it generates many other communication skill questions along the lines of "Do you also do...?" I am of course happy to help if it is within my skillset.

Is this shameless self-selling? Yes, but in a non-aggressive and non-annoying way. I humbly suggest that, if you want to market yourself and your business successfully, you learn to promote yourself in a similar non-annoying but engaging manner.

How can we put some intriguing questions into the mix with our *LuxPets* and *Mighty Dynamite* examples?

LuxPets is a service and product provider aimed mainly at pet owners and, whilst not everyone has a pet or larger animal, most of them know someone who does. You should use your intriguing questions to get people engaged so asking a straw poll works well when talking to a small group of people. You could try something like:

"Have you ever noticed how much time it takes someone who truly loves their pets and animals to find great suppliers and care specialists?"

This type of question does not specifically ask if they have pets and if not they will often think of people they know who do have them. If they are pet owners they will be interested straight away. Allow a bit of time for reflection and possible answers to your question.

I would consider following this up with a statement like:

"In fact, the number one concern for the majority of our clients is finding supply businesses which care about animals as much as they do."

It neatly answers the question for your audience, despite anything they actually said, and positions you nicely for the rest of the narrative. The more you make the elements flow together the more natural and comfortable you will become over time

Suitable intriguing questions for Mighty Dynamite would follow a similar line.

"What do you think is the number one complaint of most modern sales and marketing managers?"

This is a question that anyone in business can think about. Even if they are not a sales or marketing manager they will still understand and empathise with the many problems all modern managers face. You will usually get a good response to this question and if someone says *"time spent doing activities that ought to be delegated"* or similar, then this is your ideal opening.

I would follow up with a statement something like this:

"Right, we find that their number one complaint is doing lower level activities, which should be delegated, which encroaches on the important functions the manager should be doing.

These activities, however, are vital and still need to be done by someone."

This moves you nicely along to the introduction for your sales training and process outsourcing section. You have raised the problems you can solve right into the awareness of your listener and this makes them seem much more important and real to them. They will either have a need themselves or possibly be aware of someone else in this exact situation. They are now engaged and listening to see how you can help; whereas if you had simply listed only what you do they may never have engaged on any useful level.

Bear in mind that *LuxPets* and *Mighty Dynamite* are fictitious scenarios and the real world does not always work in quite the way that you might want it to.

My point here is that intriguing questions work well and engage your audience straight away. They are a powerful tool in your networking (and sales) toolbox. You can ask powerful intriguing questions at any time during your conversations. Come up with a range of questions that cause your listeners to think about the issue you are addressing. They should be in line with your values and beliefs and most importantly they should suit your delivery style. Spend some quality time developing your questioning skills. I will cover other powerful value elicitation questions and questioning techniques in Chapter 6.

What's so special about you anyway?

Why are you so special? Why should I refer you? Why should I recommend you and your business over all the others that offer broadly similar products and services? Why should I even listen to your introduction?

This section is vitally important to you and your success.

What does make you and your company different from all the other companies out there?

Can you find a unique beneficial result or unique selling point (USP) that clearly and compellingly sets you apart from everyone else in your business sector or location?

There are many ways to be unique. People will place value on many different things. You have to pinpoint and exploit the one that will engage your ideal client and get the point across clearly in your networking message to make sure that your ideal client hears about you or is referred to you via a contact.

For example, are you the only one in the area providing these products or services? Are you the only one to offer mail-order in this market? Are you an exclusive agent for an in-demand product? Do you have the best after sales support or guarantee? Do you have the best discounts? Are you bigger, better or friendlier than everyone else?

The modern world is noisy and you have to be able to differentiate yourself from everyone else. Being different will make you memorable. Being memorable will get you referred and will make you the profits you need to succeed.

We could add a bit to our *LuxPets* introduction now:

"LuxPets is the only pet transport company with a 24/7 pick-up and delivery option for sick animals and we are linked up with every on-call vet in the three county area. We can become your own private animal ambulance and our customers love the secure feeling this gives them."

This is a compelling USP for any doting pet or show animal owner and it delivers a superb emotionally beneficial result. Even someone who has no pets or animals can relate this benefit to their own lives and need to care for their loved ones. If your own ideal client hears this message directly, or even indirectly by referral, they will be hooked. It will be extremely memorable and so will you be.

Suitable versions for *Mighty Dynamite* might be:

"We are the sole UK agents for Sales King CRM software. Sales King is the only enterprise level CRM system that not only tracks your sales pipeline, generates your sales documents and manages all your proposals but also keeps tabs on your sales team's training programme and even suggests training interventions based on live field performance. It will make any sales manager's life a dream and even pays for itself within six months."

Or this alternate version:

"We are the only company in the UK to provide you with a one stop service for all your sales training and all your sales process design and tracking. In fact we are the only company in the UK that Sales King trust with their industry leading CRM software. One look at our FTSE 350 company testimonial list demonstrates that working with us has been a brilliant decision made by many successful sales managers."

The USP is the UK exclusive partnership with a popular software company. Whilst both versions give logically and emotionally beneficial results; they make them compelling in slightly different ways.

The first version indicates how much easier the sales manager's dream life will be simply by adopting the exclusive CRM software as well as mentioning rapid return on initial investment.

The second version appeals to and demonstrates the ease of decision making involved and the security of choosing to work with the same company that many other successful managers chose.

Take the time to find your USP and present it in such a way that it will appeal readily to your ideal client's values.

What's your story?

Long before the invention and general use of the written word, we humans have used the story as the vehicle to transmit our knowledge and our history through the generations.

Humans are hardwired to enjoy and identify with stories. We are pattern generating creatures and the nature of a story satisfies the need to make connections for ourselves.

We remember important parts of our own history in story form. We also remember other people's stories better than lists of facts.

Think about this concept for a minute or two. Remember the last time you wanted to find out about a friend's holiday. You asked them how it went but you didn't expect a laundry list of dusty facts and figures; you expected a story of how it went. In fact, if you were asked about your last holiday you would likely remember it in a wholly sensory format and then relate a narrative of the images and sensations you recall.

Stories and narratives are therefore extremely powerful tools for you to use in making your message highly memorable and sticky.

So doesn't it make sense to include a story about what you do and why you enjoy it so much? I think so.

You need to design a short narrative that captures the true essence of your business and, much more importantly, why you like doing your job which is what makes you personally unique, special and memorable.

People buy from people after all so you need to be at least as memorable and likeable as your products and services, if not more so.

Initially I would recommend putting this narrative at the end of your introduction as it will be more memorable that way. You will have left your audience with and engaging story before handing the verbal baton back to them with a query about their business or businesses. There are of course no rights or wrongs here, only options.

As a first example to illustrate the power of this technique we could add a short narrative piece to the end of our *LuxPets* introduction:

"Since I was a small child, I'd always dreamed of working with animals but becoming a vet was never an option for me. Nowadays, the look of delight and gratitude on the faces of my customers when we get their cherished family pet to the emergency room in time, then bring them home again later as good as new, is an even better reward for me. Like I said earlier, I think I might just have the best job in the world.

What is it that you do?"

This puts you right up there at front and centre as an interesting and useful person to know and deal with. I've made you up but I'd still like to meet you. You sound wonderful.

Seriously, this narrative segment absolutely qualifies as a story. You overcame the problem with becoming a vet and it has a happy ending too. Your clients and their pets are in it as characters with their own problems and happy endings. It doesn't have to win any awards but it does need to be effective and memorable.

It has a more emotional rather than logical bias to it but this is deliberate as you are aiming primarily at appearing caring, passionate and emotional to appeal to your ideal client.

Now, I've made up this person's story but I'm thinking that if it was you then I would definitely like to meet you as you sound fabulous. That's the power of a good story.

For *Mighty Dynamite* you could use something like the following short case study:

"Now, I've seen my share of tangled and broken procedures in my time, big and small, but when we helped out John Smith over at Consolidated Widgets, and I know he won't mind me telling you this because he mentioned it in a testimonial for us, their sales process looked like a plate of spaghetti.

They had sales people actually sitting next to each other in the same office with no idea which customers the other one was dealing with. They could have made 10 separate sales calls to the same customer and completely missed another 9 and wouldn't have known because of poor communication. Can you imagine the mess? Their staff turnover rate was going through the roof and their sales income was tanking. They needed our help.

I personally worked with them for just 6 weeks to scope, install and commission a bespoke sales and training system for the entire organisation. They were delighted.

Six months on and staff retention is in control, sales are way up and the system has been fully paid for. They are still delighted and I'm still dining out on that project.

What is it that you do over at XYZ Incorporated?"

This illustrates a number of narrative sales techniques that can be highly persuasive and memorable. This again is definitely a proper story. It has a hero and other characters, problems to solve and another happy ending.

It has more of a logical rather than an emotional bias to it and therefore a different emphasis than the *LuxPets* story. This is deliberate as you are aiming primarily at appearing competent, effective and professional to appeal to your ideal client.

It could almost stand on its own and would certainly allow you to shorten some of the earlier parts of your introduction if you were stuck for time.

It clearly illustrates your organisational ethos and the beneficial results you offer, mostly logical with some emotional ones. It drops in a big name client that was delighted with what you did which will establish credibility and illustrate the type of clients you work with; large and small with a large one illustrated here.

You are portrayed as an experienced expert with many big industry contacts. You work quickly and effectively and obviously enjoy the work. You have demonstrated that you can work with the client and identify the metrics that will prove the success and return on investment.

You provided a vivid visual metaphor in the form of a plate of spaghetti and you asked an engaging question that brought the audience in again at about the mid-point. You even joked about how well you did without seeming unduly boastful or burying people in the actual details.

All this and more is achieved in less than 200 words which included the nice open question at the end. Bear in mind that at usual speaking rates those 200 words equate to about a minute and a quarter. Wow, that's a lot of ground covered in less than 200 words. Those few words are doing a phenomenal amount of work for you in the mind of your audience.

Could you convey this amount of memorable company and personal detail in any other way quite so succinctly? I certainly couldn't and you don't need to try.

Let a narrative do the heavy lifting for you.

If your narrative or story is compelling and detailed enough, it can work extremely effectively on its own and form your entire introduction. People will definitely remember you for that style of message.

If you can deliver a case study type narrative that fully illustrates your core business offerings as beneficial results for your prospect, shows your unique selling points and demonstrates your personal enthusiasm and passion for your business, then your message is going to be a real winner.

Bringing it all together for the first draft

So after all that work what do we have to offer as a first draft run through?

Here is the full first draft version of our *LuxPets* introduction and it assumes you have initially introduced yourselves to each other and therefore know the name of the other person and the name of the company that they either own or work for.

"Have you ever noticed how much time it takes someone who truly loves their pets and animals to find great suppliers and care specialists?

In fact, the number one concern for the majority of our clients is finding supply businesses which care about animals as much as they do.

I love animals of all kinds and I love people who love animals. I think I might just have the best job in the world.

LuxPets is a one stop shop for all your pet or larger animal needs allowing you to focus on simply loving and enjoying your faithful friend while everything else is taken care of.

LuxPets is the only pet transport company with a 24/7 pick-up and delivery option for sick animals and we are linked up with every on-call vet in the three county area. We can become your own private animal ambulance and our customers love the secure feeling this gives them.

Since I was a small child, I'd always dreamed of working with animals but becoming a vet was never an option for me. Nowadays, the look of delight and gratitude on the faces of my customers when we get their cherished family pet to the emergency room in time, then bring them home again later as good as new, is an even better reward for me. Like I said earlier, I think I might just have the best job in the world.

What is it that you do?"

The above introduction is 245 words long. At an average and relaxed speaking rate of 150 words per minute this will take you a little over a minute and a half.

Here now is the full first draft version of our *Mighty Dynamite* introduction and it again assumes you have initially introduced yourselves to each other and therefore know the name of the other person and the name of the company that they either own or work for.

"What do you think is the number one complaint of most modern sales and marketing managers?

Right, we find that their number one complaint is doing lower level activities, which should be delegated, which encroaches on the important functions the manager should be doing.

These activities, however, are vital and still need to be done by someone.

Our fantastic service benefits essentially sell themselves and I'm the lucky one who gets to make people happy they discovered them.

Mighty Dynamite Sales Training can take over all your training and process design activity, allowing you and your key people to fully concentrate on their vital marketing and leadership functions, which will in turn keep you moving forward as a thriving profitable business.

We are the only company in the UK to provide you with a one stop service for all your sales training and all your sales process design and tracking. In fact we are the only company in the UK that Sales King trust with their industry leading CRM software. One look at our FTSE 350 company testimonial list demonstrates that working with us has been a brilliant decision made by many successful sales managers.

Now, I've seen my share of tangled and broken procedures in my time, big and small, but when we helped out John Smith over at Consolidated Widgets, and I know he won't mind me telling you this because he mentioned it in a testimonial for us, their sales process looked like a plate of spaghetti.

They had sales people actually sitting next to each other in the same office with no idea which customers the other one was dealing. They could have made 10 separate sales calls to the same customer and completely missed another 9 and wouldn't have known because of poor communication. Can you imagine the mess? Their staff turnover rate was going through the roof and their sales income was tanking. They needed our help.

I personally worked with them for just 6 weeks to scope, install and commission a bespoke sales and training system for the entire organisation. They were delighted.

Six months on and staff retention is in control, sales are way up and the system has been fully paid for. They are still delighted and I'm still dining out on that project.

What is it that you do over at XYZ Incorporated?"

The above introduction is 393 words long. At an average and relaxed speaking rate of 150 words per minute this will take you a little over two and a half minutes.

There are many areas for improvement for these two first drafts and we will take a critical look at this aspect of your message development next.

Mark Twain is reputed to have said:

"It usually takes more than three weeks to prepare a good impromptu speech."

This brilliant tongue in cheek quip is remarkably accurate and in our case we need to edit and polish our material for our introduction so that it appears natural and fresh.

Does all this mean that we will be reciting a carefully crafted mini-speech script regardless of our audience and circumstances? How will that come across as a natural, fresh and memorable introduction?

The point of all this preparation work is to ensure that you get the basic framework of your business and business networking introduction correct for yourself. You will then have understood the real benefits that your business actually offers and how best to relay this vital information to your ideal client in a compelling and memorable way. If you don't understand what you do then how will your audience?

These two first drafts are not a bad start but they have been initially constructed and written to look good on paper and may be too difficult to actually read aloud with any confidence. They may also sound a bit odd or contrived when spoken aloud to someone else. In the next three sections we'll briefly look at some editing tips to refine them a bit and make them easier to say, tips to make you seem more natural when delivering them and also ways to keep your material and your attitude to it fresh. The aim is always to ensure you are always memorable and compelling and ready to promote yourself and your business to your ideal clients at any time, wherever you are and despite whatever you are doing at the time.

The next three sections will cover ways to edit and polish it, deliver it spontaneously and keep it fresh and natural.

Polishing and editing

One of the best ways to check the readability of a passage of text is to print it out, read it aloud and record it. A cheap camcorder works exceptionally well for this.

If you find yourself stumbling over any pronunciations or phrases that seem overly complicated then take out your red pen and correct them. Repeat the recording and review process until you are happy with it.

Close your eyes and listen whilst placing yourself in the position of your audience. Is what you are saying interesting and engaging? If not rewrite it so it becomes interesting and engaging. Test it out on friends and relatives to see if they understand it. Do you use filler words or repeat any words and phrases too often?

Try turning off the sound and watching your body, hands and face. Do all your gestures appear in line with your message? Do you exhibit any strange or repetitive movements? You want people to listen to your message and not focus on your physiology too much so this is a worthwhile exercise.

Read the message in the way that is most comfortable for you and write that down. It is your script and your business after all. Is there any industry related jargon that may confuse your audience? Can you read it all in a relaxed way and does it make you feel proud about what you offer? This is your personal introductory message so you might as well get comfortable with it; you will be saying and hearing it in many different ways for quite a while.

Be ruthless when editing but remember that it will always be a work in progress. When you use it live and people always appear to ask the same clarification questions you may want to add a section that answers those specific questions and points during your introduction. This is the power of feedback. Constructive feedback is your friend and ally.

To provide you with an example of how I would do this, I have edited the two earlier first drafts to suit my style of presentation. It may not be to your taste. Take some time and try editing each of the first drafts into a form that would suit your style of delivery; it is an interesting experience.

"We wondered why pet owners spend so much time and effort choosing the right care specialist and we found that the major concern for our clients is finding a business which cares about their pet as much as they do.

I love animals of all kinds and I love people who love animals. I have the best job in the world.

LuxPets is a one stop shop for all your pet or larger animal needs allowing you to focus on simply loving and enjoying your faithful friend while everything else is taken care of.

LuxPets is the only animal care specialist with a 24/7 pick-up and delivery option for sick animals and we are linked up with every on-call vet in the three county area. We can become your own private animal ambulance and our customers love the secure feeling this gives them.

When I was small, I always dreamed of working with animals but becoming a vet was never an option for me. Nowadays, the look of delight on the faces of my customers when we get their pet to the emergency room in time, then bring them home again later as good as new, is an even better reward for me. Like I said before, I have the best job in the world.

What is it that you do?"

This message is now a mere 222 words long and yet it still delivers the desired information. It takes me a little over a minute to say it aloud now in a relaxed voice. I have replaced some words that I found tricky to say and also removed some weak phrases to make it more powerful overall.

The most significant change was to the question section at the start. After careful consideration, I felt that this question could prove to be a potential stumbling block. If your audience does not have pets, or cannot immediately think of anyone they know with pets, they may not give the question any thought at all. This will lose their engagement straight away.

I have altered it and shown you another technique which involves a useful hypothetical question both posed and answered in the same sentence. Here it implies that *LuxPets* care enough to investigate their client issues and act on the answers. This is a powerful technique that you can use in your own introduction.

Here is the next phase of the Mighty Dynamite introduction, again edited purely to suit my own style. Try it for your own style.

"What do you think is the number one complaint of most modern business managers?

We find that their number one complaint is that they are doing lower level, but still necessary, churn activities instead of the important business functions they should be doing.

I'm the lucky one who makes those managers happy when they discover there is another way.

Mighty Dynamite can take over all your routine sales training and sales processing activity, allowing you and your key people to fully concentrate on their vital leadership functions

We're the only one stop sales system and training provider in the UK that Sales King trust with their industry leading CRM software. Our testimonial list demonstrates that working with us has been a brilliant decision made by many highly successful sales managers.

When we helped out John Smith over at Consolidated Widgets their sales process looked like a plate of spaghetti. They could have made 100 different sales calls to the same customer and completely missed another 99 and wouldn't have known because of poor internal communication. Can you imagine the mess? Staff turnover was flying and sales income was tanking. They needed help.

I personally worked with them for just under 6 weeks to scope, install and commission a bespoke sales and training solution for the entire organisation.

Six months on and staff retention is down, sales are way up and the system has been fully paid for. They are delighted with Mighty Dynamite and I'm still dining out on that project.

What is it that you do over at XYZ Incorporated?"

This is now down to a mere 262 words which can be comfortably read allowed in well under two minutes. For me it still provides interest and information and will definitely interest your ideal client.

I have left the opening questions broadly intact this time as they will pre-filter anyone who isn't a busy manager or someone without a reasonably large sales force in their organisation.

Though it has been edited substantially the story still does most of the hard work here and still works well in demonstrating your work and approach.

Don't memorise it internalise it

When developing your introduction, it is tempting, especially for those new to the process, to try and memorise it word for word and section by section.

This is a big mistake. Word for word memorising of any script is purely for actors only.

Consider the potential stumbling blocks of using a word for word memorised introductory script. If you miss out a section you risk missing out information that your audience may need. If you stumble over a word or phrase and try to correct it you will quickly give the highly rehearsed nature of your script away and it will destroy your credibility. You will also struggle to vary your message delivery if a dialogue starts and your audience asks a question you have not rehearsed an answer for. The list goes on and on and most scenarios do not end well.

The way to perfect the delivery of your introduction is to internalise only the essence of what you want to say. This means you can design each section of your introduction as key points then cover all the points and key phrases that you want to get across and flesh them out as appropriate to the current situation.

What you won't do is stumble by missing out particular words or forgetting the order of the script. There is no set in concrete running order or specific wording other than your key points and phrases. If you think about it from this perspective you will realise that you can't actually get anything wrong. This can take the pressure right off you.

Internalising your points and phrases this way rather than trying to memorise them will allow you to sound much more natural when talking with people. They will not feel that they are being given a scripted lecture.

Feeling relaxed and in control of a flexible and fluent business introduction means that you can carefully listen to and respond appropriately to what the other person says; which in turn makes them feel valued and appreciated.

There is a place for some memorising, however, and the general memorising of certain key phrases or particular stories, that convey a powerful business message for you, is definitely to be recommended. You can then use these all-purpose building blocks in a variety of situations and they will always sound fresh if you deliver them with enthusiasm and passion.

I make use of aide memoires to help me internalise the main points of any message and I also use this style of aide memoire to help me internalise speeches, stories and training modules. As an example here are the internalisation points I might remember for one of my personal networking introductions and also the two draft introductions previously developed for *LuxPets* and *Mighty Dynamite*:

- Good leader speech - presentation - sales [all asked as hypothetical questions]
- Three bad versions of whatever questions I used above [all asked as hypothetical questions]
- Noisy world – communication skills needed
- I help business engage with audiences
- Future paced - working with me for tools and techniques
- More prospect, leads & clients in one hour than 3 months
- How is your current business building? [Asked as a straight question]

Note that this list only has to make sense for me. No one else will see this running order. It is written in a shorthand form that I can easily remember and understand. I can put in whatever I want for the actual wording other than a few favourite and powerful phrases that are favourites of mine. This format gives me wide latitude for adjustment and always sounds natural. Even stopping and thinking briefly after each point helps me as I am visibly demonstrating that it is not scripted and I sound more natural. So will you.

Here is my version for the *LuxPets (LP)* example:

- Pet owner time spent finding suppliers? [asked as a hypothetical question]
- I love animals – best job in world
- LP is your one stop shop – you just enjoy your pets
- LP has 24/7 animal ambulance – secure feeling
- When I was small –vet not an option – customer delight better – best job in world
- What do you do? [Asked as a straight question]

Here is my version for the *Mighty Dynamite (MD)* example:

- Manager complaint [question and answer bit]
- I'm lucky statement
- MD can take over sales process and training churn
- MD is one stop provider with Sales King software + testimonial list
- JS at Consolidated Widgets spaghetti story and the happy ending
- What do you do? [Asked as a straight question]

Note again that these are written in a form that I can understand. You should develop your own easily remembered shorthand for your introductory messages aide memoires. I don't think these are hard to remember and they give you a certain amount of latitude to move segments around. For example, if at an event someone didn't ask you what you do but instead asked you about your most interesting challenge or ideal client. You could say something like "Well, let me tell you a quick story about that…" and go into a version of your John Smith narrative. This scenario has the added advantage of you being able to elaborate quite a bit because they invited the telling of your story.

This is the paradox in that focused preparation can appear as flawless and dynamic spontaneity when handled correctly.

What can you do with your introduction? If you have not done so already, take the time to develop a flexible dynamic one in this fashion.

Bear in mind that if your audience is clearly not interested or engaged in your introduction it is not necessarily the fault of your message. They may well understand it but there might not be a suitable connection for you or they are not particularly interested in talking shop at that time. You can't hope to please all the people all of the time as the saying goes. Accept it, smile politely and cut short your introduction then both move on to talk to other people in the networking event or simply talk about other things if you are in a social setting.

Many people dread being interrupted but with regard to your networking message, being interrupted by someone asking a relevant question is almost always good news. This shows they are interested in what you have to say and are either seeking clarification of more information. This has now become a dialogue.

Keep in the moment, keep the momentum and follow the new conversation. You do not have to get back to your introduction and finish it. It has already achieved its purpose so move on. You are now connecting with the other person. Give yourself a pat on the back because you've done a first class job.

Variety is definitely the spice of life

Nobody is immune to boredom. If we hear the same thing repeated over and over again it can and does get boring. If we say the same things over and over again that will bore us.

Someone at a networking event may never have met you before so your introduction or story will be fresh for them in terms of content and originality.

However, if you are becoming bored with your own offering, even if it is internalised and not memorised, this will come across in the delivery. Disinterest and boredom are as infectious as passion and enthusiasm. Your audience will not engage if you are not engaging. You will become memorable but not in a good way.

The trick is to have numerous ways of delivering many of your key business points available to you. Keep your messages fresh by changing the content within the well developed and successful structure we've created. Keep things dynamic by keeping things up to date and experiment with new ideas now and again. Be creative and if the new thing doesn't work then try something else.

Go much further in your preparation and internalise several of these business offering narratives. You can then select the perfect one each time you network. This will keep you interested in your own introduction and you'll come across in a much more enthusiastic manner.

You can use different stories or anecdotes to answer specific questions that others may ask you. Because they are pre-chosen and designed to illustrate the benefits of what you offer they will serve you well, raise your business credibility and make you highly memorable. The more options you have at your disposal the more flexible and adaptable you will be. You will also feel more confident and in control of the situation and this will help you relax.

Some powerful and helpful questions to ask yourself when preparing your collection of all-purpose and useful message segments are:

- What do you love about your work or business and why do you love it?
- What gets you out of bed in the morning?
- What is your best/worst client experience?
- Have things ever gone wrong? What did you learn from it and how did you bounce back?
- What pivotal event in your life got you started in your business?

- What recent client-centred experience portrays all you do for people in the best light?
- What other business offerings can you introduce via a story segment?
- Do you have brief interesting case studies that show your benefits rather than merely tell your features?

Always ask questions. Listen to other people at events and social occasions. Do they have techniques that you could use or adapt? Be a lifelong learner and keep it fresh.

Learn to listen extremely well

You will, I hope, be aware that the skill of listening is vitally important. You will have been told this many times over the years. The term active listening is now commonly used to describe the most useful aspects of interpersonal listening technique. Everyone generally acknowledges these statements and believes they are true.

But, and let's be brutally honest about this, how many of us actually do listen well? Do you actually listen to other people as deeply as you could do? What is active listening anyway?

Do you respond to what was actually said or simply what you would have liked to have been said? There's a big difference.

During the majority of conversations and in particular at business or networking events, most people are so pre-occupied with thinking about what they are going to say next, that they often neglect to listen to the person opposite at all. If they do listen, it is only with cursory attention.

If you are actually talking or thinking about content for your next turn at talking; you cannot be actively listening to the other person.

This can mean that vital information gets lost. Two people, who may have had the potential to be wonderful connections, will simply not engage due to poor listening and attention skills. Remember not to make assumptions about the person you are talking with. They may be of colossal benefit to you in terms of who they connected with; despite your first impressions of what they say they do. If you listen deeply and well you will pick up important clues that others may miss.

Asking powerful open questions of the other person is also hugely beneficial to you and I will cover more about this in Chapter 6. For now, be aware that open questions are those that encourage the other person to think a little and supply a more detailed and information filled response than a straight "Yes" or "No."

When you are comfortable with your core business offering, both the benefits that you can provide to others and also your skill in communicating this information, you can relax and actually listen to the other person.

People love to talk about themselves. Let them and actively encourage them. People will give you valuable information either verbally or non-verbally.

Have you ever been talking to someone who is constantly looking past you or around you to see who else is available? It is not pleasant so I recommend not doing it to others. Nowadays, I generally drop people who do this in double quick time. They are not the best people to spend any of your valuable time with.

When the other person is talking you should focus all you attention on them. You should make frequent eye contact, smile often and nod your head now and again. Make appropriately timed encouraging noises to keep them talking.

When they have stopped talking and expect you to speak you have the advantage that you can easily show how well you have listened and understood their message by adapting your response to suit their values and needs. This is a mightily impressive skill which makes you highly memorable to people who don't practice it. When you meet those people who already do this you will both recognise a kindred spirit and there will likely be a solid future connection for you both. It is pleasant to be both listened to and understood.

Do you listen as well as you could? It is a skill well worth acquiring and it is a skill best learned through application and practice.

I will finish this section with an instructive observation. We generally have two ears and only one mouth and it is well worth using them in that ratio.

I realise have spent a huge amount of time and page space on the business message generation and communication aspect of your networking skills because, as previously stated, I believe it to be the most important aspect of all. I therefore make no apologies for all this material; it will serve you well in many other areas of your business and private life.

Chapter 5 - Effective preparation prior to organised events

You have decided to take the plunge and go networking at an organised event. You have hopefully generated and practiced your introductory message and you are confident that your business has much to offer.

This section will cover some essential and useful preparation work that you should do prior to attending any event. This will ensure that you get the most out of your networking experience.

The host with the most

I want to look at the role of the business networking group host in a bit more depth. The reason that it is hugely important for you to get this part right is that you need to feel comfortable with the host and be aware of the benefits they will bring you or supply to you on request.

There are two main types of host. The smaller networking businesses are generally hosted directly by the network business owner. When the network business is a large concern with multiple venues and schedules, there will be area or specific location event hosts. Some groups are franchisees of larger organisation.

Whichever category the host falls into, their hosting skills and contact knowledge are extremely important to you. They can and should be a fabulous information resource and are generally more than happy to help connect you within the group but, perhaps more importantly, they should have a wealth of business contacts in other groups and in your local area.

To be acting as group host, or indeed setting up and running a networking business, they should be business networking experts themselves.

You must also like the host as you will be interacting with them a lot during the period of your membership and whilst you are at the meetings. They have to pass your personal ABC test.

Host skills and likeability are two of the most important areas to check out when you're researching groups to join. Talk to the host in detail before you commit to joining any group. If the current membership roll is not on a website then ask to see a physical copy of the membership list to get a feel of the people that are already members. You obviously cannot expect to keep it but you can certainly expect to check it out first. Remember you need to network where your ideal clients network. It can be expensive to get it wrong.

If you do join the group, make a good connection with the host and access all those contacts; it will pay big dividends over the long term. Get to know this person well and make their life easier by completing things such as administration requests and your meeting payments ahead of time. They will then be well disposed to help you as a result.

If you provide help to your better quality Level C network connections, and I recommend that you do this frequently, in the form of links, articles, event information, etc… consider including your host as a natural part of your Level C network. They in turn will make you a natural part of their network and not merely a general networking group client.

Work with the host to help them understand what your business benefits are all about and also who your ideal clients or referrers are likely to be. With this important information the host has the ability to introduce you to, or seat you next to, potential connections that are most likely to be of benefit to you.

If the host cannot or will not do this it could be for several reasons: The networking group is simply too small, the other people there are not at the level you require or in the right business sector, the host does not understand you or their other members well enough, etc...

If any of the above hit home as being current issues for you then you might need to look carefully at the group you are in and decide if another group may be better.

If you find that you have made a mistake by joining a group that is not right then take it on the chin as a learning experience. Many people are tempted to keep going for the rest of the membership period in order to get their money's worth but this can cost more again in meeting fees for which you are not gaining anything. With time often being more valuable than money, I would recommend that you find a better group for you and invest your time and money in that one instead. One good referral, client, connection or referral partner will more than cover the lost money from the poor group. I will talk in much more detail about this in Chapter 8.

Who is going to be there?

Another useful facet of knowing your group host, and/or their meeting administrator, is the ability to find out ahead of time which specific businesses or individuals will be there.

Knowledge of specific attendees is potentially incredibly important to you. If this concept of targeted networking seems like overkill when you could simply go with the flow and treat every event as an adventure, here are some scenarios and options you might like to consider before you dismiss the idea:

You may have some valuable resources or information that they will benefit from. They will appreciate you doing this in person much more than using any other medium and you will be that much more memorable. Being memorable in a good way leads to those referrals.

If their company is one you would like to work with you can do a lot of prior research and have some quite specific things to discuss with them. You can tailor your benefits offering to match their current needs and this will rightly appear highly professional on your part.

You can also request your host to place you on a specific table. This could be to target a specific business or person or to put you on the table that will yield you the most benefits in terms of potential quality connections. Your time is, or should be, valuable and they should be happy to oblige whenever possible.

Conversely, you can ask not to be placed with certain people or companies. You may have nothing in common with them and consider it is a waste of networking opportunity for both parties. You may simply physically dislike the person and want to spend no time with them at all. This is an option that many people do not consider but it can save you a lot of time and boredom over the long term.

With paid for business networking, don't forget that it is your time and your money so take control of how you spend both.

What you wear speaks volumes

Now, I am the first person to agree that we would all do much better by not relying on superficial things like clothing or appearance when we make our instant judgements about other people.

The reality of our world, however, is that we do rely on superficial things. It is even said by some that we form a strong impression of someone in the first seven seconds of meeting them. I am not certain if this figure is actually true but I do know from personal experience that our first impression forming time is extremely short.

If we take a few minutes to consider the benefits of the strategy we might even appreciate the value it can bring us. The world is busy, noisy and potentially dangerous.

From the times of the earliest humans there have been benefits associated with deciding quickly: Is that animal dangerous? Is it tasty? Is that other human going to kill me? Is that other human a good mate? Is that rustling noise good or bad? Etc…

Nowadays the scenarios are slightly different but the questions are essentially variations on the same themes: Is that person dangerous? Is that person going to be good for my business? Is that person trustworthy? Is that person dressed as I would expect? Is that person going to mug me? Is that person a potential mate? Etc…

It makes sense, therefore, to maximise the factors that can create a good first impression and minimise the factors that don't.

You would expect a police officer on duty to wear the appropriate uniform, business people from different sectors expect certain types of clothing to be worn by others in that sector. This uniform identifies people as being serious about membership of the group.

Being memorable is one of the goals of networking but you don't want to be remembered for the wrong reasons.

Take care to find out the appropriate uniform expected by your target audience and wear it. That way you can use the whole of the short time available to you to make an impactful impression rather than trying to correct any poor impressions caused by the wrong clothing or inappropriate outfit. Notice that I used the term inappropriate. If it is an informal networking group don't show up in a sharp suit as you will stick out like a sore thumb and possibly make other people feel uncomfortable. You will be noticeable for all the wrong reasons. Likewise, for a strictly formal event, don't show up in jeans. If you are in any doubt then clarify the dress code in advance with your host.

There are of course many ways to be memorable and still fit the bill. Men, for example, can wear bright colourful neckties and ladies can wear bright scarves and jewellery. This is perfectly acceptable in most normal business circumstances; so take full advantage. Becoming known for something that amuses or cheers people up is a fantastic way to be memorable.

Personal grooming

For similar reasons to dressing appropriately, your personal grooming has to be of the highest standard you can manage at all times. Remember that first impressions count; for and against.

If you think that mentioning this aspect of your appearance is over the top, believe me when I say that I have been on the receiving end of some amazing smells, dandruff covered jackets, sharp nails and horrendous bad breath from people trying to impress me with their business skills. If those people cannot look after themselves a bit in areas that are fairly easy to maintain, how much care and attention will they lavish on my business needs?

Keep your hair in a suitable style and make sure it is clean. If you have dandruff; use an anti-dandruff shampoo. Keep your fingernails in good condition; clean and neatly trimmed for the men, tastefully decorated and not too flamboyant for the ladies. Brush your teeth or try chewing some of the new style teeth friendly chewing gums right before, but please not during, an event. If you have dental trouble that is causing bad breath then go to the dentist and get it checked out. Garlic is nice to eat but not as a second-hand smell.

None of this stuff is rocket science. If you were going out to dinner with a date and you were trying to impress them, I would hope that you would pay close attention to these small details. It would be the same for a job interview or an important sales meeting. Treat your business networking in the same way.

As with so much in life, it is the little things that make a big difference. Your attention to detail and consideration for others is demonstrated by your care of your own personal grooming. It does get you noticed. Be memorable for all the right reasons.

Plan your journey

It is almost seems too obvious to mention here and I don't want to appear patronising, but planning your journey is vital. One of the most annoying things for a good host, who has worked hard at promoting and planning an excellent event, is for people not to show up and the other attendees are also expecting a certain number of businesses to be in attendance.

If you miss an event that you told people you would attend, for any reason at all, it can appear unprofessional and it could also cost you money, time and stress. To miss it due to a simple journey planning omission is doubly annoying.

Networking groups often meet in new locations as a means of creating or maintaining interest and also for taking discount advantage of venues that want to promote themselves to other businesses.

One big advantage in getting to a venue early allows you to meet people as they arrive; the host benefits from this and so do you.

Getting to an event late is a fantastic way to destroy your carefully prepared mind-set and make a poor first impression with the host and the other networkers.

I personally hate being late for anything so, if you are like me, here are some simple checks you can go through: Determine the exact location of the venue – I love my satellite navigation system. Have some loose change ready for any parking fees. Listen to travel reports and have some alternative routes planned. Check the weather and dress appropriately in case you have to walk any distance. Set off in plenty of time as this allows for any delays. Get there early if you can for time to relax and prepare things like your mind-set and any notes you might need. Etc...

What could you do to make your networking journey run more smoothly?

Have a checklist for the other essentials

I have placed several useful event preparation checklists in the virtual appendix for this book on my website. Link information is in the Appendix section right at the back of the book. Feel free to use them or even adapt them for your own particular needs. If you design a good one I could use then let me know.

It can be extremely annoying to forget simple things like business cards, mobile phone, pens, money, meeting location and time, etc... I have managed to forget all these things and more and it certainly annoys me. If you are someone who likes to live on the edge in a random chaotic fashion then I wish you good luck and enjoyment. If you are not then I recommend that you design and use your own checklists to ensure that you don't forget anything for your event attendance.

You will be more relaxed and event ready and therefore you will be much more effective at the event.

Get your networking mind-set right

We have discussed the importance of a good quality and positive mind-set earlier in the book. Immediately before the event is the time to ensure you are ready to go in the right frame of mind. This is important stuff to pay attention to because if your mental and emotional state are not as good as they can be your physiology and other non-verbal communication will betray you and you will be ineffective at the event. This is poor use of your time and money.

Getting there early and relaxing to prepare is a definite advantage for you. Listening to calming music on your journey may also help. Repeat any positive and affirming mantras you have developed to relax you still further.

It is always a good idea to have a specific goal for what you want to achieve at the event. This could be to meet a specific potential client or targeting a certain number of quality connections established for follow-up.

Now, visualise being successful at the event and achieving your goal target. Visualise delivering your introduction perfectly and naturally to a receptive audience. Visualise meeting your intended potential client or referral partner and hitting it off right away. The choice of visualisation method is yours but visualise – it works. You will be fully relaxed and looking forward to the event.

Make last checks of your hair, shoes and clothing. If you wear it, check your make-up. You are now ready to go.

Embrace the moment and, most importantly of all, enjoy it.

Chapter 6 - Being highly effective during networking events

You have prepared well, you are at the venue and now you have to walk in and connect well with a group of fellow business people. This is the point where a great many people get extremely nervous. Their minds are full of such questions as "How do I introduce myself and make small talk with complete strangers?"

One of the key points is making a great first impression so let's dive right in.

Making a great first impression

As I've said previously, the current reality of our world is that, rightly or wrongly, we rely on superficial things to inform us how to behave and respond when encountering new people. We also form this strong first impression of someone in an extremely short space of time.

I have mentioned clothing already and wearing the right uniform certainly helps. Make sure it is clean, pressed and as lint free as humanly possible.

There are many other ways you can make a good impression before you have even said a word of networking introduction inside the room.

There is sometimes an administration person or greeter in the hallway at these organised events. They sort out things like signing in, issuing name badges, table assignments, etc… Introduce yourself initially to them and make a point of chatting with them a little. It will relax you and they will then be happy to help you if you need further assistance. They sometimes also have responsibility for table assignments so getting to know them well can give you an edge if you want to be placed with certain people at an event.

How you enter the networking room itself is important to assist you in making a good impression with the other people.

If you are naturally confident and happy already with how you approach people and commence to chatting and conversing easily, then I applaud you and wish that I had the same levels of aplomb and social grace. You do not need to change anything and if I ever meet you I will be looking to model your skills.

For myself and the rest of you that aren't so confident or socially skilled, I will be offering some ideas, tips, strategies and thoughts to help you begin the task of mingling and beginning conversations with complete strangers.

Always enter the room looking relaxed, highly confident and in control. Walk in at a nice steady pace with your head held high and a big smile on your face. The big smile is important. People always pay attention to new arrivals and seeing someone with a face like a wet weekend will not have people rushing over to say hello.

I recommend stopping a few feet inside the door and remaining still and quiet for a couple of seconds whilst letting your eyes scan the room. If you see someone you know well, I suggest moving straight over to talk to them. If you don't see someone you know well I recommend going straight over to the event host and either chatting to them or being quickly introduced to someone they are talking to already. If you don't see anyone you know at all then head to the drinks table which gives you an activity and time to take stock until you feel more relaxed. This will also give you time to survey the room. You might even strike up a conversation with someone else who is doing the same thing.

My wife and I love people watching and I would suggest that you become a keen student of people's behaviour as well. You can learn a lot about people from their non-verbal communication and interactions. Without being too obvious, spend some time watching people in restaurants, queues, business events, meetings or any other similar situation and see what you can learn from their non-verbal behaviour. It can become quite an addictive activity but please don't become a full-blown stalker or voyeur as this will get you into a lot of trouble.

For you as a networker, paying attention to some simple group dynamics will pay huge dividends. The concept relies on analysing simple body language and determining if a group of two or more people is an open group or a closed group.

Anyone on their own is of course not a group and, unless they are obviously doing something private such as telephoning or reading intently, they should be easily approachable and will likely welcome the attention. Quite why anyone would be taking a phone call or reading intently when at a networking event is beyond my understanding but I have to say that I have seen it with my own eyes many times. It does not present a good first impression in my opinion. If you are that busy or important that you have to take or make a call then perhaps you shouldn't be there at all. In a similar vein, if you are doing something obviously solo, like reading intently, you're signalling that you want to be left alone which is not a recommended tactic for mingling with others.

When two people are talking they can adopt two basic stances in relation to one another. If they are deep in conversation and obviously interested in what they are each talking about you may notice that they are facing each other squarely. A group of three or four would form a similar triangle or square that had no obvious entry point or physical invitation to join it. These types of group structure are called closed groups.

If you stood next to such a group and tried to make eye contact or speak to one of the participants and gain entry into the conversation, you would struggle. The most likely outcome is that you would be ignored and you would have to move on. This is an embarrassing situation to say the least. It could be worse if you actually annoy the people concerned. Either way don't approach closed groups. It doesn't happen often but if all the groups appear closed I would suggest talking to the host and asking to be introduced. The host then gets to be the pushy one and you get what you want with no annoyance or enmity directed at you.

If you see two people having a less serious chat and they are standing at an angle to each other there will be space to one side of them. This is a non-verbal invitation for someone else to join the group. This is referred to as an open group. Larger groups will also exhibit this open structure or will easily open up to accommodate you if you do happen to stand next to it. They are non-verbally inviting you to join them.

It is the individuals and open groups that you should look to join and engage with when mingling at an event. If you want to talk exclusively to someone then you can close the group yourself by altering your stance appropriately.

There are many other non-verbal clues and techniques relating to group dynamics and interpersonal interactions that are well beyond the scope of this book, but simply identifying open and closed groups will be extremely useful to you when trying to striking up conversations with people at any social event.

104

If you are thinking that all of these manoeuvers, group dynamics analyses and social gambits are incredibly clinical, artificial and won't fool anyone, consider this argument. It can be daunting when you arrive at an event, especially when new to this type of part business and part social networking. Having reliable tactics and a broad plan to work from will get you started on the right path and will enable you to relax. Feel free to work out your own strategies and methods. We are all different after all and we all play out our own strategies. The alternative is to creep nervously into the room and stand alone for a while in the hope that someone will come across and all your troubles will be over. This might happen but the odds are generally against it.

One blindingly obvious, but often overlooked fact, is that whilst the majority of people at an event or social gathering may look cool, calm and collected, they are almost certain to be in the same boat that you are. They will simply have learnt better coping strategies. Some people will look as confused and lost as they actually feel. You do not want to be one of these people. Learning useful social coping strategies will pay you dividends. Is it easy? The answer is no I'm afraid. However, it gets easier with time and more importantly practice. Find someone you know who is exceptionally relaxed when meeting people and copy their mannerisms and style until you feel more comfortable and relaxed. Social skills are best learnt the old-fashioned way; by trying them out as often as you can.

Let's talk about the actual moment when you meet someone else for the first time. People will quickly size each other up when first meeting and they will each have a different preferred indicator of compatibility.

For me, the handshake is still the de facto standard of appraisal when I first meet someone, male or female. For example, if I was meeting you for the first time, a good firm handshake, a smile and good eye contact would give me the impression that you had friendly confidence and would also show me that you were not aggressive or pushy. You would be someone I would spend some time with in order to find out more about you.

What constitutes a good handshake?

Do not be a "Mr or Mrs Bone Crusher" as this is guaranteed to make you memorable for all the wrong reasons. Conversely, being "Mr or Mrs Limp Grip" is equally unappealing. All you need is firm steady pressure and a couple of gentle up and down movements. Practice with a friend if you have to, but try and get it right. Watch out for sweaty palms if you are nervous as this is a bit off-putting for others. Keep your hands dry by surreptitiously blowing on them or possibly carry some tissue paper in your pocket to dry them off. Everyone gets nervous but if you are aware of your reactions then you can prepare for them and present yourself as well as possible using a little pre-planning.

Here is a little trick that you may like to try if your hands tend to get mild perspiration building up. When you wash your hands with proper soap and you are rinsing them off, leave a little of the soap you used on your hands and then dry them with this soap still in place. You will find this thin soap barrier will absorb minor perspiration and keep your hands dry. Please do not try this if you have skin that is sensitive to soap.

Avoid the use of greasy hand creams too, as this can be highly unpleasant for other people and they won't thank you if it gets on their expensive business clothing.

As a male, when meeting ladies for the first time, my jury is still out on air-kissing or even actual kissing. Many ladies will prefer a firm gentle handshake to being kissed by a stranger so err on the side of caution. For the ladies, it is also a good idea to avoid kissing the men until you know them a little better. It may surprise you to discover that some men are actually shy and may well be put off by what they may see as aggressive female behaviour. Become aware of the prevailing culture of your business sector and group first and I recommend always erring on the side of caution until you get to understand what people expect and like.

Your smile is also a huge part of you being liked and making a good first impression but please make sure it is genuine. Your whole face lights up when your smile is genuine. It looks false and unappealing when it is forced. Smile as much as possible but try not to overdo it. You may take on a slightly crazed look after a while and people will begin to back away.

Eye contact is an interesting topic and one that gets many people confused. Eye contact should be frequent yet brief. This implies innate confidence, interest in the other person and a relaxed attitude. Staring hard at someone is often taken as either aggression or craziness and both should be avoided when trying to socialise for obvious reasons.

If the person has a name badge it is difficult not to look down and read it. Don't stress about this as everyone else does it and you can make a joke out of the situation to break the ice. If you can read the name in advance you have a sight advantage so speak first and use their name after giving yours. This is polite and shows social grace.

Take a nice deep breath, smile, look the other person in the eye, take their hand in a firm but gentle handshake grip then introduce yourself in a clear voice and ask your opening question.

"Hi, my name's Andy Pope, what do you do for a living Bob?"

Get in first

You are networking to promote yourself and your business. You are hopefully excited and enthusiastic about your business offerings and services. Now that you are aware of some excellent ways to frame your introduction and beneficial results, it might be tempting to wade right in with your networking introduction. Stop! This is a mistake.

Even if you do all the right things, regarding the offering of benefits and an engaging and persuasive story or narrative, you have still made a basic error and minimised your chances of success.

Consider this alternative approach and the potential benefits it has to offer to you.

Introduce yourself to the other person and ask them what they do first. It's that simple.

The question posed at the end of the last section is an excellent place to start.

"Hi, my name's Andy Pope, what do you do for a living Bob?"

The benefits for them are that someone has shown an interest in their work and business and allowed them time to talk. Most people simply love to have favourable attention focused on them and to talk about themselves and their work.

If they are the introverted and quiet type then be patient and use some powerful questions to find out more about them and their business needs. I will talk about these powerful questions and how to use them in the next section.

The benefits for you are that you are instantly likeable in the other person's eyes and, much more importantly, you will have an excellent idea of what they do and what they might want in business. Ask your powerful questions, apply your active listening skills and read their body language; they will tell you a lot about their values and unspoken needs.

When they have finished talking about themselves you will find it is far easier to adapt your introduction based on your new knowledge. You can promote and focus the beneficial results of what you do far more effectively when you know something of the other person's business. They will remember you.

That's it. Be polite and let others go first.

If you haven't noticed yet; most experienced networkers will always invite you to go first. They do it because it works.

Powerful language versus small talk

We are all aware of what small talk is and many of us dread it. Lightweight meaningless statements and chatter about the weather or the traffic. Have you ever been in a conversation at a party and the conversation simply died away because no-one could think of anything useful or interesting to say? It's not pleasant.

Fear not, because business networking conversations need not be like this for you. There is a way to control the situation, gain all the information you need and all the while make the other person feel good about you and the whole process.

Despite my comments earlier, some small talk is actually useful and necessary; it is the oil that lubricates the social gears. It is always worth testing the waters with some general chatter to see if the other person is in the mood for a more in-depth conversation about their business. They might simply be having a bad day and don't want to talk. Save yourself time and politely move on. Because they are in a bad mood doesn't mean you have to waste your day.

If someone is in a bad mood, never allow yourself to be dragged down with them into their pit of despair. Do not feel that it is the polite thing to stand and listen to them whilst they do a karmic dump and unload all their bad feeling onto you. You are there to network not provide a therapeutic sounding board. Let them get on with it themselves. You have other business to attend to.

If you have invited the other person to start off talking about their business or work and they have given a typically brief laundry-list style description of their business, you have two options. You can accept it as is and go into your introductory presentation or you can take the time to find out more about them first. I strongly recommend you take the second option.

This is where you should start to use powerful talk or powerful language.

Powerful language means keeping statements to an absolute minimum and questions to a maximum. Not just any old questions either. They need to be powerful open questions that can elicit valuable information. Open questions are ones that require more than a simple "yes" or "no" answer.

The key is to keep the other person talking. Most people are happy to talk about what they enjoy. The fact that you are showing interest and paying attention by asking questions will make them even happier. When they are talking and you are listening carefully the treasure you seek will be uncovered.

Here is a list of some suitable powerful questions. Fill in the blanks with their business sector or role. Use appropriate variations where necessary because the questions have to be in the style that suits you and it will also serve to keep things fresh for you and the other people there.

- How did you first get into the business?
- What advice would you give to someone starting out in the business?
- What aspect of the business do you enjoy the most?
- What makes you stand out from all the other businesses?
- What is your best customer experience ever?
- What is the biggest challenge you currently face in the business?
- What are the latest growth trends in your sector?
- Who or what is your ideal client or project?
- What is the biggest change you've seen in the business?
- What do you enjoy doing when you're not working?

I don't recommend asking every one of these questions one after the other or you'll sound like an interrogator. Pick a few you like or invent your own similar ones. They are powerful questions because they are open and invite thoughtful considered answers from the other person.

Don't merely carry straight on with a new question. Ask follow-up clarification questions in the form of *who, what, where, when, why* and *how*. This shows you are paying attention and interested in learning more. One powerful question and a number of subsequent follow-up questions may elicit all the information you need to know.

If they ask you a question at any time then you must obviously answer but be brief and get back on track quickly with a power question or follow-up of your own. Get them talking again.

It is tempting to leap in with your own war stories from time to time but resist the urge. If things go silent, let the silence continue and don't allow yourself to start talking. The other person will carry on soon enough.

You will be perceived as an attentive listener and a fine communicator. You will be able to adapt your message to suit the values and interests of your connection with much greater ease and accuracy.

How many people should you talk to?

The old saying that quality is better than quantity is perfectly applicable to business networking.

The general idea of the ABC approach is that at the Level C of your network you will have a relatively small number of contacts that you are confident enough to trust and cooperate with to work on your behalf and likewise you will work on their behalf in the same spirit.

It takes a while to build these solid Level C relationships. You have to move through the A and B levels to get there.

At any networking meeting, I recommend spending a brief period of time with each new group member, or person you haven't yet met, to find out the basic details about what they do, in what industry and also with what specific level of client. Can they be of help to you and can you be of help to them?

Getting to the meeting early helps in this regard as you can meet and greet any new people and have your quick initial chat.

Once you have met these new people briefly, I recommend having a more in-depth chat with only two or three of the more promising or interesting connections.

This will allow you to connect with them far more easily the next time you both meet and take the conversation a bit further without starting from scratch.

If all this sounds overly cynical or too calculated, please bear in mind the fact that everyone has to make best use of their time. Time is extremely valuable to everyone so you are actually helping yourself and other people by adopting this attitude.

Talking on a purely superficial level to too many people at an event inevitably results in confusion and is essentially a complete waste of everyone's time. You will be seen as simply a social butterfly. Many people will like you or find you entertaining but you will be an ineffective networker with far too many acquaintances.

Mind your manners

Manners are still incredibly important in much of life. Sadly, they are rapidly becoming something of a forgotten art and are considered old-fashioned by many. Our modern lives, however, would quickly descend into chaos without them.

As already stated, in the context of business networking, it is vitally important to make a great first impression. It is also vital to maintain that good impression and build on it.

It is sometimes all too easy to let your guard down, especially when others are being less than polite in terms of their language and behaviour. Don't succumb to the temptation and join them. Someone is always watching or listening.

A much less used and appreciated tactic involves using good manners to your deliberate advantage when networking.

If someone is boring you or simply hanging around too long, you can offer to get them a drink and/or introduce them to someone else then quietly move on.

If you want to meet someone specific you can again take the role of host and offer some refreshment. The powerful influencing force of reciprocity, or the desire to repay favours, will provide you with their favourable attention.

Politely introducing a new member or guest to someone will ensure both parties will be fully aware of your advanced social and networking skills. This is all good publicity from your point of view.

Manners can therefore be highly useful as well as socially acceptable.

Meet your contacts but mingle on

It is always nice to meet with people you know well at an event. It is also something of a safety blanket and can limit how many new people you can meet at an event.

If you are new to business networking and you find that meeting and interacting with new people is a mental and physical drain on your energy then there is a real risk of you staying in your comfort zone and remaining in conversation with people you are friends with for the whole meeting.

If you genuinely have that much of importance to discuss with them you should have a one to one business meeting away from the networking event.

You should always meet up with any pre-arranged contacts and discuss your news and commonalities as well as the specific topic you wanted to meet up for. You should then carry on and mingle to chat with new people. It is a networking event after all and not a social.

Another factor to consider is the contact that you are chatting to all the time will almost certainly want to network further for their own benefit and get the best out of the event. You will be sorely trying their patience and politeness by latching on to them to make yourself more comfortable and relaxed. You might find yourself on the receiving end of a polite and sometimes not so polite brush-off.

You may have time to waste on this occasion but they probably don't. You may get a clingy reputation and word gets around. You will indeed be memorable but for the wrong reason.

Try setting specific time limits on these encounters and force yourself to meet other people. Set a target of perhaps meeting three new people per event for example. You will be doing everyone a favour and you will grow in confidence with each new meeting.

What if you are on the receiving end? How do you get rid of a clingy attendee? Politely introduce them to someone who is passing by and then pop to the loo or get a drink. You are then free to mingle and network as you intended. Remember to be nice whenever possible but be protective of your valuable time and use it effectively.

Be the introducer

You are already aware that any good business networking event should have a knowledgeable host who should know who everyone is and something about their business.

The host should always try and introduce you to suitable contacts and they should also try and move people around to meet more than one person or group.

At any reasonably busy event the host is going to be stretched in their ability to carry out all the necessary introductions and will therefore rely on other people doing their own introductions, introducing others and ensuring sufficient mingling takes place.

A useful technique for you as a networker is to become such an introducer and mingle-master.

If you have been chatting with someone for a couple of minutes and wish to move on and meet others, you can simply offer to introduce the other person to someone else you already know. You are then free to move on.

You may also want to meet someone specific that you haven't yet been introduced to. Introducing a newer person to them can be an effective icebreaker and also allow you to naturally strike up a conversation with your desired prospect.

The newer people will see you as an experienced and friendly person, the established networkers will recognise you as a proficient social communicator and this is all good advertising for you.

The host will hopefully appreciate your efforts but more importantly you are taking control of your networking experience. Taking full responsibility for and control of your environment is the only real way to get on in networking, business and life in general.

Help the quiet ones

We have all had the feeling of being nervous at social or business gatherings. I certainly still get nervous before presentation, trainings and speeches. This is natural and it shows a desire to do well for yourself and your audience or other guests. Even the calmest and highly self-assured individuals feel nerves of varying degrees before a social or business event depending on the importance of the occasion.

If you have ever been married or attended an important interview you will know what I mean. Networking events, especially the initial ones, can sometimes overwhelm otherwise calm individuals.

Some people never get over this initial bout of nerves and they are always the ones stood alone or at the outer edges of the group.

Many people leave them alone which makes the situation worse. They may leave the group never to return. Everyone potentially loses.

If you take the time to talk to these people and bring them into the various conversational groups you will possibly make solid connections and form valuable future business relationships. You may miss valuable buried treasure if you do not make the first approach.

You will gain in confidence and the whole group will see you as an effective and friendly networker. Being nice makes you feel good.

You could even agree to be a mentor to quiet group members but I recommend only offering this service if you are asked for help by the host or the networkers in question. Anything else may make you appear pushy or arrogant. Helping others is a superb way to learn and improve your own skills and confidence.

Of course, there are some people for whom no olive branch or offer of help is acceptable. They may have completely the wrong idea about networking or simply be quiet because they dislike the group and will leave soon anyway. They may have a major personality disorder or a huge private life problem. Test the waters carefully before diving in and don't try to force anyone to do anything they don't want to do.

Watch the nibbles

Organised business networking events are put on in many formats and at many different times of day.

Some are based around breakfasts or lunches and have a sit down to eat format.

Networking whilst sat down and eating is perfectly fine. However, if the table host picks you to go first, your food may go cold. The real trick is to eat first then talk. Offer to be the table host and choose someone else.

Most events will have liquid refreshments of some kind as a minimum. These are also fine; a cup or glass can be held easily which leaves a hand free for shaking with others. If air-kissing is definitely your thing you can still do it while holding a single cup or glass but try not to spill it.

Some networking groups think that providing buffet style food is the way to go. Apart from possible cost savings, I have never seen any real benefit in doing this.

As tasty as the food undoubtedly is, I would recommend that you leave it alone for networking purposes.

Many people grab a drink and a snack; mainly because everyone else is doing it. You will have no hands free and, unless you are a professional juggler, you will struggle.

It gets worse. You will likely spray crumbs on everyone as well as having bits and pieces of food in your teeth and on your clothes; not a good look for anyone. I've been on the receiving end of buffet spray and it is not pleasant.

I have also seen many white shirts and dresses ruined by the bright red mini-pizza sauce stain or similar. Generally, the itinerant hobo look is never on-trend at business networking events. It will of course get you that all important memorable status but is that what you want to be remembered for?

Personally, I steer clear of buffets and I strongly suggest that you do the same. I also tend to avoid networking groups that constantly put buffets on but, if you enjoy them, be aware of the potential pitfalls.

Take a few minutes to imagine how others might view your efforts at conversation with a plate full of food and drink in hand. Is that the lasting impression you want to leave them with?

There is a growing trend for early evening business mixers that are held in café bars and trendy city centre pubs. There are also themed events based on all-day partying. These are billed as networking events but I if you do attend I recommend that you treat them as purely social events.

I personally do not believe that alcohol and serious networking go well together but if that is your thing then be aware that these events are available and appear quite popular with certain people. If you do go then the same networking tips I recommend for other events apply here with the added caveat of suggesting that you try to avoid getting hopelessly drunk.

Exchanging business cards

We should all have good business cards.

If you don't have them then you need to get some as soon as possible. There are some cheap options available to you online but I recommend that you invest in having them professionally designed and printed.

The business card is a way of leaving someone with your contact details so that they can get in touch with you or pass your details on to a potential customer.

Some people spend money on flashy or cleverly shaped business card designs in an attempt to be more memorable. In my opinion, unless you are a printer or graphic designer, this is a waste of time and money. Your message will make you memorable. Stick to a classic, professional and tasteful business card to complement your business image.

Your business card is not something to push into the hand of everyone you meet at an event. There is a huge amount of noise out there in the business world and your card will simply become more noise if it is an unasked for offering. You may well be remembered but it will be the wrong sort of memory association and your card will likely be thrown away at the earliest opportunity.

You should only swap cards with people you feel you want to keep in touch with or people you feel you can introduce to others.

Likewise, you should only present your card to others if they express an interest in contacting or referring you in the future.

Unless there is a real reason to keep a business card, I will generally throw it away. I am not alone here. How many business cards or advertising flyers have you collected that went straight in the bin?

If I want to keep the personal or business contact details I will find ways to usefully record them and the card is then binned.

So, don't merely hand business cards out to all and sundry. You will devalue your business status if you do. Have you ever handed a business card to someone you knew didn't want it? Give them only to people you want to deal with and that might want to deal with you; no one else.

Arranging and agreeing to follow-up meetings

This is an area that many novice networkers make mistakes. I have personally learnt my lessons the hard way.

Most people at business networking events are genuine and honest business people; people you will enjoy meeting with, working with and referring on to others.

There are some individuals who attend networking events with the express intention of selling directly to people at the event. They are obvious and easily identified. I have already mentioned them and cautioned you against being perceived as one of these people.

Sadly, there are also some people who are more subtle and calculated in their sales approach toward you. I class them as nothing less than predatory and I will not associate with them in any way, shape or form once I have identified them for what they are. They deliberately seek out new and inexperienced network attendees and they will chat with them at length to appear as a valuable resource and contact. They will express visible and obvious interest in the other person's business model and plans. This interest is naturally extremely flattering for the new networker. The predator may well try and arrange a meeting then and there or, again more subtly, catch you at the end of the meeting and suggest it then.

This cynical predator is merely lining you up for a hard-sell session for their own business offering and how it will benefit you and your business. They may also try and shoehorn the benefits their offering into a joint venture proposal with you. The benefits will of course all be for them.

I don't want to paint a bleak picture but merely to warn you that these people do exist. I have had these experiences and I tell them to you now so you don't have to learn the hard way.

One simple way to sort out most follow-up meeting issues is to establish the purpose of the meeting in advance. I will illustrate this with an example experience from my past.

I was approached a few years ago by an individual who expressed huge interest in some communication courses I was planning. He explained how important communication was in his line of business, which had no bearing on mine by the way, and wanted to arrange a meeting about including some of my seminars in a business training day he was planning. This was what I desperately needed early in my business plan. We set a meeting location and time and I drove out to meet him. What did I find when I got there? He was cheeky enough to try and sell me on the idea of including him talking about his business for a couple of hours in my communications course. He actually seemed surprised when I gave him my full, frank and unprintable response. I drove home mad at myself for being so naïve. He had lied to me and if I had asked for more details ahead of time this lie would have been apparent and I would have saved a lot of money, time and grief. I was thinking too much with my ego and desire to succeed. The interest in my business was flattering and he took full advantage. It did teach me a valuable lesson which I now pass to you.

If someone is genuine about a meeting with you that they feel will provide a win-win outcome they will have no problem specifying the purpose of the meeting to you if you ask. It's that simple. If they can't offer a good compelling reason or you do not see value in meeting then thank them and diplomatically decline the offer. You are not a charity and it is not necessary to accept every request simply to be nice and not upset people. It is business you are in and not a popularity contest.

Likewise, if you want to meet with someone, make sure you have a valid useful reason and specify it up front when you ask them. Do not be surprised or offended if they diplomatically decline. Your reason may not be compelling enough for them, they may simply not have the time to see you or they may not like you or your style; it happens so get over it. Either way you will both have saved time and money.

I recommend thinking through your reasons for a follow-up meeting carefully. On reflection, you may decide that the option to meet is not a good one and you can abandon it easily. If you still see value in the meeting then present your ideas and options via an e-mail a day or so after the event. This takes the immediate pressure to respond off the other person and they will give your suggestion a more thorough examination. You will also have more control over the various meetings and projects you are developing.

In general, make sure you are careful to honour any promises you make at events. I will discuss this in much more detail in Chapter 7, but if you promise to follow up with a meeting or information, make sure you do. Do not waste people's time or fail to deliver on your promises.

You may have time to waste but the other person may not. Your throwaway line about getting together for coffee may mean nothing to you but be as good as an arranged meeting for the other person. Word gets around and your hard-earned credibility may suffer.

Be yourself at all times

I hope this doesn't appear to be too obvious but I have seen too many people at networking events trying to be someone or something they are not.

People buy from people they like and trust. It is highly annoying to try and deal with someone you thought you liked and trusted but they turned out to be presenting a fake image to the world when you first met.

This applies equally to you and all your dealings with the world.

If you are a one man band that's fine but don't tell anyone you are a bigger company and try to fake it. I have seen many people try this and fall flat on their faces.

By all means, team up with like-minded or complementary businesses to form groups or associations that offer a wider range of services. I recommend this approach and use it myself with a lot of success. Make sure the connections are in place prior to promising the services. Please don't make any big sales or contract promises then scratch around for help with it. This approach will only end in tears.

Don't claim to be a super salesperson, a dynamic introducer or a world class deal maker if you are simply unable to do any of these things. In fact, don't claim to be anything you are not. It is simply not worth it.

It is tempting when first starting out in business to agree to, or claim to be able to do, all manner of work in order to get started and earn some income. It is good to push yourself and stretch your skills in order to grow but don't overreach or promise too much as the cost in the long run is much greater in terms of your credibility and reputation.

If you have not carried out a task or work operation before, but are keen to try it, I recommend letting the other person know this clearly so that they can make the decision to try you out, rather than you assure them you are an expert and try to wing things. You will be found out soon enough. Be prepared to recommend someone who can do the job properly to them and they will be highly impressed with your professionalism and probably offer you other more suitable work in the future.

I have heard some people talk about and recommend the "Fake it until you Make it" approach. I don't subscribe to this concept as the costs of failure are high and it is incredibly stressful to keep up a false image of yourself and your abilities. As a professional business person I recommend that you say only what you can do and then do what you say you can do. This approach builds credibility and allows you to sleep easily at night. I mention an incredibly simple but powerful technique called "Acting as if" in Chapter 11 but only recommend using it in connection with your own networking mind-set and other self-development applications. Never pretend to be something or someone you are not in order to fool or deceive someone else.

Always remember that we are all unique individuals. We all have strong areas and areas that need attention. We do not all get along in a harmonious celebration of joy.

If you are at a networking event and you don't like someone you meet, don't agree to meet them or even swap cards; part amicably. If you try and build up connections with everyone you meet you will be piling up problems for the future. You will not like everyone and everyone will not like you; that's life.

Be true to yourself now and you will be more credible to others later on.

Chapter 7 - Achieving effective networking follow-up

You have finished the networking event and you are hopefully heading away feeling that it was a job well done. Hopefully you enjoyed it, you met some interesting people and you formed some promising business connections. If it was your first networking event then I would like to offer my congratulations to you; may it be the first of many similarly successful networking meetings.

So is that it? Do you leave it at that and hope that the work and referrals pour in? Not quite I'm afraid.

In order to maximise return on your effort and investment there are several techniques you can use to follow-up and increase your ability to be favourably remembered and referred.

E-mail but don't spam

A well-proven and non-aggressive follow-up technique, beloved by most knowledgeable and successful salespeople, is to write a courtesy "nice to meet you at xxxx event" e-mail. I recommend mentioning some personal detail relevant to your conversation or their business that shows it is not a template e-mail. Send this email out on the same day or at the latest within one working day of the event. This demonstrates that you were indeed sincere in your expression of interest in them and/or their business and you are also willing to take the time to connect via personal e-mail. You are not trying to sell them anything or even ask for a meeting. If you had discussed a possible meeting, I recommend saying that you will investigate some calendar options and that you will contact them again in a couple of days to take things forward regarding meeting up. This shows you as being considerate, not pushy and that you are not desperate. The recipient will remember you and also have your details on file in case they lost or threw away your business card. If you promise to follow-up with another e-mail then make sure you do.

It is also perfectly acceptable, essential if you promised to do it, to send a follow-up email to someone you met to provide some information or answer a specific question regarding your services or their business needs. You could even politely ask if that person would like to receive your (hopefully interesting) business newsletter, but do not send it until their written permission is given.

I am talking here about following up after business networking events. You are building business relationships at this stage. You are not selling to people. Sending sales letters to sales prospects on a sales mailing list you have developed via other means is acceptable but it is the subject of a different book. Do not put your networking connections on these sales prospect lists unless they specifically ask to be placed there or they buy from you in some other capacity and get on the list that way.

Spam or unwanted e-mails are threatening to clog up the entire internet. There is only one thing worse than getting spam mail from strangers and that is getting spam mail from someone you met briefly at a networking event. They have taken the introduction and business card as tacit permission to start sending you mailings and newsletters or special offers every week or month. They are relying on the fact that, because you physically met them, you will put up with this nonsense and simply be too polite to block their intrusive marketing efforts. Personally, I would quickly put them on my spam list and then generally ignore them as a serious business connection.

I have had the normally acceptable "nice to meet you at xxxxx event" note format arrive from someone only to find that, when I opened it, it was filled with sales pitch material. This is unacceptable and it is spam. Don't be tempted to do it. It will cost you much in goodwill and business over the long term. This behaviour is essentially the same as selling directly and openly at a networking event and is not the correct way to achieve success in the relationship networking and business referral world. It is unacceptable predatory behaviour. There are actually new laws against spam so it is very important to get buy-in from customers and also allow them to unsubscribe easily from any sales lists they give written permission for.

So, please do not become a networking spammer as your credibility will suffer far more than you will ever gain from potential increased sales to the networking group. This potential spam threat is another reason to be careful about whom you pass your business cards to at networking events.

Follow-up meetings should have a purpose

It is fair to say that following-up with contacts is one of the most important things you can do in business networking. Certainly, if you promised to follow-up, then you should definitely do it.

I have mentioned this earlier in the book and expand on it a bit here because it is so important. The most important thing in my opinion is that you follow-up properly.

As stated, a same or next day "nice to meet you at the xxxxx event" e-mail is a nice and acceptable touch. A more specific follow-up note or email should, as a minimum, provide the information or help promised. It could also politely invite the person to subscribe to a newsletter or possibly get together with you for a one to one meeting. It is this last bit that I want to talk about here.

The one to one meeting can be the cause of so much wasted time that many people can be quite reluctant to accept the invite from people they have only recently met.

I learnt the hard way that the follow-up meeting can be a timewasting, annoying and expensive activity.

When I started out I was so pleased to have any attention regarding business that I would meet up with lots of people for a one to one discussion. As a result I have been on the receiving end of more than my fair share of timewasters.

To add insult to injury they would often cite a need for my services then turn it round to a request for me to buy from them; I have even travelled considerable distances to meet them. I recounted such an annoying expedition earlier. I quickly learnt how to avoid this situation.

Modern business seems to run on meetings and they are rife in the corporate world. They account for large amounts of lost time and money. I have even heard them described as the "Practical alternative to work." I don't know about you but my time is valuable. I cannot afford to waste it in pointless meetings.

There must therefore be a specific and defined purpose and desired outcome for a meeting of any sort and networking one to one follow-up meetings are no exception.

Successful salespeople learn to pre-qualify their sales prospects to see if they are motivated to purchase, able to purchase and are looking at the right solutions before they spend valuable time pursuing lost causes.

You should pre-qualify requests to meet with you in the same way. It is not arrogance or conceit it is good business practice. Your time should be valuable to you; do not waste it on pointless meetings. If you want to meet people for social reasons, that's fine and I wish you every enjoyment.

For business reasons, I recommend that you find out exactly what they want to meet you for. If someone doesn't immediately specify a compelling and valuable purpose to me as part of an invite to meet them I will openly ask them for one; if it does not appear good enough or simply does not suit me, I will diplomatically decline the invitation. If I need more time to think about it I will request a more detailed proposal via e-mail. Their time may not be valuable but my time is. How valuable is your time?

Likewise you should do the same for people you want to meet with. It is common courtesy in my opinion. E-mail them and explain to the person why you want to meet and what is potentially of benefit to both of you. They can then accept or decline as appropriate and nobody gets upset.

I work with many other business people and complementary businesses in creative ways that enhance all our prospects. I like collaboration. The reason I like networking so much is that I can meet and get familiar with a wide range of people with a wide range of business offerings. I cannot often discuss my ideas or proposals with full effectiveness at the actual networking events so I spend a lot of useful time in follow-up meetings with potential business collaborators. I take great care to ensure that the people I meet with are fully aware of the purpose of the meeting and the potential benefits to us both before we agree to meet.

If they accept your meeting request, arrange a suitable meeting place and time and get confirmation that it is agreed by the other party.

I would then design a meeting agenda and send it to them for scrutiny. This shows you are serious and also thoughtful regarding the best use of everyone's time. Your credibility goes up with every demonstration of professionalism you can provide. A short agenda is relatively easy to put together but sends a powerful message to the other person. They now have the option to amend the agenda and add their input. You have begun a dialogue before the meeting; always a good thing.

You will probably still be annoyed by timewasters now and again and not all meetings turn out well, despite the best of intentions, but you will have a much higher success rate than most with some pre-qualifying, pre-planning and a professional approach to the whole process.

Keep your promises

Credibility in any business or profession takes a long time and a lot of effort to build up. It is no different when trying to build credibility as a business networker.

What exactly does credibility mean? Credibility is the quality of being trusted, convincing and believable. Do you do what you say you will do? Does your business deliver what you say it delivers? Are you the professional that people expect you to be?

It can be all too easy to destroy your hard earned credibility and one of the easiest ways to do this is by failing to keep your promises.

What constitutes a promise anyway?

You may believe that a promise is only a promise when the word is specifically mentioned in the exchange. Anything else is only a throw away comment. For example, "We must get together for a coffee and catch up."

The person you talk to may well believe and live by the ethic that if you say you will do something then that constitutes a solemn promise. In the above example they will be expecting you to sort out a meeting to have a coffee and a chat.

They will likely consider you a time waster and highly unreliable when you don't call. You will lack credibility in their eyes. You meanwhile have probably forgotten the whole thing yet wonder why you get a cool reception at the next meeting.

It can work the other way too. How many times have you called someone up to arrange such a meeting and it turns out they are too busy or want to put it off until some far off future date? You will have them down as a timewaster.

I recommend you be careful with the statements that you do make. If you treat them all as potential promises you will find yourself paying much more attention to the outcome scenarios that you are creating.

Saying only what you will do and doing only what you say is a brilliant attitude to adopt when running both a business and also your life in general.

If you say you'll follow-up then do it. If you say you'll send some information then do it. If you say you'll pass on their details to a contact then do it. If you say you'll do something then do it.

Take some time to consider this question. In either your business life or your private life, have you ever used a throw away comment similar to the example given above? If so, what do you think the other person thought about that comment? What did they think about you when they felt let down?

Create or get a Contact Relationship Management (CRM) system

Business networking is all about building relationships and referring of your business contacts to others as well as you being referred to others by your own business contacts.

It will become quickly apparent to you that, even with careful selection of contacts, you can start to build up a huge amount of information and business relationships. You would benefit from a way to usefully store and easily retrieve this information.

I recommend that you create or acquire a Contact Relationship Management (CRM) system.

This could be as simple as a manual colour coded index card system and, whilst old-fashioned, it will work effectively for quite a while.

Depending on your level of business networking and the type of business you run you may have to move up to a computerised system.

The good news is that there are a lot of them out there. The bad news is that there are a lot of them out there. Some are free and some are paid for. I recommend talking to your business contacts and friends to find out which ones they use and like. As always, do your research.

The more sophisticated computerised systems will allow you to keep all the contact information and also track referrals to and from them. They often contain a host of other ways to process useful business information from your contact list.

Don't put every contact you meet on the system. I recommend only keeping the most likely or useful ones. You could also assign codes that determine where they are in relation to the ABC strategy model for example. You can set it up to work the best way for you and your business. If you have people working for you on your computer or IT systems, have them integrate it with your existing software to gain maximum return on your investment.

The key thing here is that you should find the method that works best for you then use it regularly and frequently to keep it up to date and earning its keep.

Keep personal notes

I recommend that you keep personal notes about your most promising contacts.

I am not suggesting that you start stalking them, going through their garbage or taking photographs of them like a paparazzi.

I am also not talking about detailed business reports or analyses of their market share or product descriptions.

What I am talking about here is that you keep some personal notes that will enable you to more easily reconnect with them when you next meet.

Now, I know my memory is not what it was, so I outsource large parts of it to notes and lists. I would be completely lost without my notebooks.

The previously discussed CRM system is a perfect location for some simple personal notes about your contacts.

Here's the thing, we all love to be listened to and when people remember personal things about us it shows they care and like us. We like people who like us; we can't help it as it has been hardwired into our systems over time.

You sometimes get on extremely well with someone the minute you meet and you feel instantly that it will become a good business relationship. The problem is that you may not see them for a while, so I suggest noting the sort of personal information that comes from the informal one to one chats with people. This information serves as an icebreaker for next time and re-establishes the relationship quickly and naturally when you next meet.

What sports do they like and what teams do they support? How many kids do they have? What does their significant other do? What things annoy them and what things make them happy? There are obviously many more questions of this type available to you.

Before you are scheduled to meet the person again, take a quick look at the CRM personal notes section and re-acquaint yourself with what makes them happy and the things they like to talk about.

The point is that when you can recall one or two of these facts and mention them next time you meet someone, your standing as a networker will skyrocket and people will remember you for the right reasons.

Do not use this information as cynical leverage to impress the other person. Use it merely to reconnect easily with them and take the business relationship further along the ABC track.

All this can come from some simple notes that you took the trouble to write down and look at prior to networking meeting.

Always be aware that there are data protection laws in most parts of the world. Even though the personal notes you keep might only refer to sports teams or hobby interests, the same laws apply. You should treat the information in the same careful way you treat all business data and comply with all relevant laws.

Chapter 8 - Reality checks and performance monitoring

Running any business on gut feeling alone is a recipe for disaster. You need to measure the effectiveness of all parts of a business in order to be able to manage them. You will already be aware that business networking is merely one marketing tool among many and as such it has to pull its weight and earn its keep like any other strategy. If you got zero response from newspaper advertising after several heavily researched and planned attempts, would you continue to invest in newspaper advertising? Why should business networking be any different?

Organised and paid for business networking can be an expensive activity if you don't monitor your financial position and investment return closely.

To do this correctly you should factor in all the networking costs involved and measure these against all the networking derived returns generated.

All the recording and analysis of such financial data may seem tedious to you, it is not my favourite activity either, but understanding exactly what is happening with your cash flow is vital to any business. Here are some things to measure.

Main Costs: These include such obvious items as the business networking group subscription fee and the per-meeting costs as well as any additional charges for food and drinks.

Hidden Costs: These costs are not always obvious and are sometimes overlooked. Some can appear trifling but can accumulate and must therefore be counted. The major hidden cost is lost opportunity. When you are networking you are not actually making any money directly for your business by selling, manufacturing, developing new products, creating designs, designing courses, etc... The argument against this statement would be that you are investing in building relationships but, until these generate income either by direct work with a contact or by referral, they do not yield actual profits at the time. What is your hourly rate? Include travel time. You should include such things as fuel for the car or public transport costs to the venue and any parking charges. You should also include the costs of any of your promotional material given out at the various events and any other applicable additional costs you can identify.

Profits generated: The basic method I use is accurate enough to determine if your networking costs are exceeded by your networking returns. Only use the profit returned on business generated by dealings with your business networking group derived contacts or referrals supplied by them. I use only received income but you can use whatever base line you are happy with. This is only to be used as a rough guide after all.

Financial position: This is simply the money in minus the money out at any convenient point in time. If it is negative then networking is costing you money. Obviously there has to be subjective analysis of the result. If you have only been networking for a short while, you would likely expect poor results until momentum builds. Monitor things regularly and check that the numbers are moving the right way. If you get big negatives, even though you have been networking for a good while, then I suggest you may need to re-evaluate your networking activity. You may need to work on and develop your actual networking techniques. You may also be in the wrong group or groups and may need to find out where your target audience and ideal clients go to network and go there instead. Your business may actually benefit much more from other forms of marketing. You may need to seek professional independent advice on how best to redistribute your marketing efforts.

Understanding exactly what is happening with your cash flow is vital to any business. We monitor most costs in business so why should networking costs be any different? Make sure that networking is not costing you money.

I am a big fan of business referral networking as long as it is providing me with what I need to grow my business and I make the income I desire. Networking can be a pleasurable activity and I have built some excellent friendships along the way. Please remember that it is a means to an end and not an end in itself. Networking is merely one marketing tool amongst many available to you. If organised business networking ceases to work well for me then I will cease to take part or invest in organised business networking. If it is not doing what you want it to do then change your methods, change your venue or change to another form of marketing altogether. It is your business and you have the ability to control how you run it. There are only so many hours in your day and you must use them wisely; run your business in the way that works best for you.

Chapter 9 - Speak up to increase your exposure

Most people hate or even fear to speak in public but they are missing out on a fabulous networking and business generating opportunity by not doing it. Are you one of these people?

Many networking groups have time built into their schedules and programmes to have a group member present about themselves or their business offerings. Some even bring in outside speakers to help educate their members about certain aspects of the business process.

Time and time again I see poor use being made of these opportunities by many business networkers. Some businesses take the option whenever they can and they use their platform time to generate remarkable business results.

Talking about your business with enthusiasm, clarity, effectiveness and a compelling message raises your game in a number of ways. Talking in public gets your message to many more people than is usual for an event, you gain instant expert status, people are impressed that you have the ability and willingness to do it and finally you can demonstrate the passion and enthusiasm you have for your business. People buy passion.

Talking well to an interested and attentive audience about your business can equal money in the bank for you.

Do you need to be an experienced, expert and professional public speaker to do this? No you don't. In the networking event scenario you simply have to be passionate and knowledgeable about your business as the audience will generally forgive minor speaking shortcomings. The more you do it the more relaxed and comfortable you will get. Keep stretching yourself; staying in your comfort zone too long will prevent further growth.

There are many opportunities to speak about your business offerings and industry insights. Check out local service clubs, local and national industry organisation meetings, industry conferences, industry or general business exhibitions and numerous other options. You could even create and run your own training seminars and these can be run as physical training events, teleseminars or as internet based webinars. When done well these activities can boost your expert status and make you the business or consultant people turn to first. It is like networking on steroids.

If you do enjoy speaking or training and intend to take your presentations further afield you will gain many more benefits but you will also need to ensure that you are an effective, competent and confident public speaker or trainer. If you are a larger employer who sends employees out to networking events and you want them to speak, make sure they are trained and competent to do it well. There are numerous ways of gaining these valuable and transferable speaking skills.

I would recommend using a first rate speaking coach or communications trainer, such as myself. You could also try joining a local speaking organisation such as Toastmasters International or similar. These are good options to take to overcome any speaking fears you may have, get you started and build up your speaking skills to a good level.

Are there opportunities to speak that you are not taking but would like to? Have you seen other business people taking the initiative and doing well as a result? I recommend you dip your toe in the water at the next available networking event speaker slot and give it a go.

Chapter 10 - Effective development of an employee networking team

Many larger businesses, for example those in the consulting, legal or financial fields, are keen to network in order to generate new prospects and clients. This is exactly what good networking is intended for.

I meet many people at networking events that are employed by these larger businesses. They are sent out like missionaries to attend the various events and spread the good word about all the wonderful things that *Conglomerated Inc.* can do for the rest of the poor benighted souls living in small business land.

The main problem with this plan is that the poor people they send out on this undoubtedly well-intentioned missionary work are woefully ill-equipped with suitable networking skills.

They are usually extremely intelligent and personable people and they are almost always a pleasure to meet but they clearly receive little or no training in the process of networking. The *Conglomerated Inc.* upper management incorrectly assumes that because they are very clever and friendly people the various staff members will figure things out and make a huge success of the operation.

Here are some of the major issues as I see them.

It is fair to say that most business people who go to networking events have a vested interest. That is, they either own their business or franchise outright or they have a substantial amount personally invested in it. This makes them very motivated to network and build their businesses. However, even the most motivated people can struggle to get the best from their networking; which is why I wrote this book in the first place.

The employees of *Conglomerated Inc.* are exactly that, employees. This means that they have far less personal investment in the process other than keeping their immediate boss happy regarding event reports and catching up on work that accrues whilst attending the networking event. There may of course be some excellent ways to incentivise the success of networking event outcomes in order to increase the employee engagement but I will leave that to individual businesses to ponder.

Larger companies like *Conglomerated Inc.* appear, in my experience, to provide minimal networking skills training for their networking employees. They seem to lack fundamental understanding about modern business networking and don't consider this type of soft skills training to be justified. They do appear to furnish the missionaries with copious amounts of company history and informational nuggets such as group turnover, branch locations, company mission statements, etc. This lack of training and experience leads the employees to merely copy the other networkers they meet; they then recite the typical laundry list of services coupled with the copious amounts of company supplied data. This unfortunately makes them extremely boring and being boring makes them memorable for all the wrong reasons. They feel bad, the people on the receiving end feel bad and *Conglomerated Inc.* gains no real benefit from any of it. *Conglomerated Inc.* might actually do better by not sending any people to these events given the pitifully low level of training support and backup they offer.

Do you work and network for *Conglomerated Inc.* or a business very much like it? Are you a director of *Conglomerated Inc.* or a business very much like it?

What can be done to sort these issues out? How can you get your employees networking effectively and also feeling good about the whole process?

The key here is to offer some appropriate training to your employees and for you to fully understand that networking is not different simply because you are a large business.

The principles of effective business networking apply equally to everyone. All the managers of *Conglomerated Inc.* might think that the raft of data regarding the size and history of the business is interesting but I've got some bad news for you – it isn't! Nobody cares. It's boring! I won't be impressed by it and I won't remember it. All I will remember is to try and avoid the next *Conglomerated Inc.* employee when they try to hit me with the same boring spiel next time. Even if they are the best company for me, I am unlikely to ring *Conglomerated Inc.* because I associate it with too many negative feelings and images. Is that the result you are after from your networking investment?

Remember that the ABC strategy applies to people not businesses. People buy from people and they buy primarily from people they like. This is important to understand, your employees are unique individuals in their own right; they are not merely a smaller version of *Conglomerated Inc.*

Whether you are a large legal firm, a large accountancy firm, a large financial institution, a large sales company or a large whatever business, each employee you send out will have a unique role within that organisation and unique work experiences to draw on. These are the things that will make them memorable and not the fact that they work for the mighty *Conglomerated Inc.*

Encourage and train your employees to network as themselves. Encourage and train them to follow the processes provided in this book. They can then develop their unique personal message and people will remember them personally and more specifically what they can personally do for them. For example, if I make a personal connection with a lawyer because they specialise in boat accident claims and I am a keen sailor, if I need a lawyer for almost any reason I will most likely remember them as a lawyer that I know and like and I will call them. Even if they cannot help me directly, because they are a part of a larger organisation, they will almost certainly be able to refer me internally and you still get the business. Your employees will also be much happier with the whole networking experience and therefore they will be more effective. A virtuous circle of positive feedback is created.

So, encourage and train all the employees to develop their individual and memorable case study repertoire and encourage them to express why they are passionate and enthusiastic about their work and careers. Believe me when I say that they will not be anywhere near as passionate or enthusiastic about your mission statement or company values.

The best way to get buy-in for any development project of this type is to let the people at the sharp end design most or even all of it for themselves. For networking training of this type I would recommend running frequent short interactive group workshop sessions to spread the word. This type of group activity can inspire and get the best from everyone if they are well-designed and facilitated. You should then hold regular internal review sessions which will allow best practice and fresh learning to be shared as well any issues or opportunities to be brought up and discussed. Team spirit will build organically and the company will be seen to be walking the walk. It is a win-win scenario and a sound investment of time and resources that will more than pay for itself over time.

If you intend to take advantage of the opportunity to use speaker slots at networking events, something I highly recommend you do, then make sure you prepare your employees for the task. Get them some high quality presentation skills coaching. Develop a slide presentation that does not send the audience into a coma but actually adds to the quality of your message. The devil is in the details and you will help your employees no end with this sort of skill development. The benefits will also ripple out and through all their work and their development as the future leaders of your business will be accelerated.

I also further recommend supporting your employees further by helping reduce any workloads that build up through time spent attending events. You could also consider some sort of incentive scheme as previously mentioned. Try asking your employees what works best for them. Remember that happy employees are more productive employees.

Chapter 11 - Final thoughts and your next steps

Develop your memory skills

People generally love two things in any conversation and you can use both to your advantage when networking.

One thing that people generally love is to talk about themselves to someone who appears sincerely interested in them. This is why it is always a good idea to let others go first in networking situations and use your best listening skills to encourage them to talk.

The other thing people love is to hear is the fact that someone remembers their name and, even better, some personal details. I have already covered a good way of remembering personal details which is via your CRM system or even a good old-fashioned notebook.

The best thing you can do is to actually remember their name. When you remember someone's name and repeat it back to them several times you demonstrate real attention and care in your relationships with others. It is quite a classy social skill to be able to make confident and accurate introductions for people you have only recently met.

I can almost hear you all crying out loud, "But it's so hard to remember people's names at events!"

I agree with you. I have to work extremely hard at it and would like to be better than I am at remembering names. It is indeed hard to remember all the names you hear when you are first introduced. It is much easier to remember names when you chat on a one to one basis.

The good news for all of us is that memorising things and people's names are skills that can be both learnt and taught.

There are many memory strategies available that allow the effective retention of people's names right from first meeting. These strategies do take time, practice and effort to perfect but, like most things in life, the more you put in the more you get out.

Be aware that if you develop your memory skills and are able to remember more names and personal information you will begin to excel in business networking and you will engage more easily, with more people and for more of the time. It is a fabulous social skill that will pay dividends in all areas of your life.

If you have a particularly bad memory I suggest you read some self-study books on the subject or attend training workshops. I have attended several courses myself and found them fantastically beneficial.

Working with a skilled memory trainer will more than repay the initial investment.

We often don't think twice about upgrading our computer software but we never think about upgrading our mental software or our social skills. Why is this?

In what other situations would you like to have more memory skills? What other mental software would you like to take to your version 2.0?

Develop good habits

Developing good habits is a useful thing to do in all aspects of our lives.

A habit is essentially any behaviour strategy or thought process that we do without consciously thinking about it. A good habit is one that is beneficial to us or to others. Bad habits are the reverse.

What are good habits for you to develop when networking?

As the author of this book and having sweated blood and tears in its creation, I would have to say that adopting and practising most or all of the techniques I have provided will help you to develop the good habits that will make you a successful networker. Of course, I may be slightly biased here.

Developing all the good habits takes time so to start you off, if I had to recommend five vital ones, I would choose these to begin with: adopting a positive attitude, pushing out of your comfort zone to enable personal growth, following up well with people after events, valuing others and listening deeply.

You will of course develop your own range of useful habits depending on your specific business and personal style.

You might adopt a highly recognisable clothing style when attending events. As long as it remains appropriate, legal and reasonably tasteful you will always be memorable.

You might send unique or highly personalised follow-up notes or cards that help endear you to others.

You might make a point of sending interesting and business relevant articles to each new contact as part of your follow-up strategy. Helping others is always a good habit to form.

Getting into the habit of using your CRM system and always prepare well for meetings will stand you in good stead.

Not all habits will be good or beneficial ones. Some will actually be detrimental to your networking efforts and it is always worth checking why you do certain things a certain way. If there is a positive outcome then do more of it. If not, you may want to consider altering your strategy. Seek coaching assistance if necessary but, however you do it, make sure you do try and do it.

So, when you have formed recognisable habits, keep checking to see that they are effective and not merely efficient ways of doing the wrong things again and again.

Seek feedback from trusted peers or friends and always seek for continual positive development of your habitual social and networking skills.

"Acting as if" and modelling

This relatively short section is aimed at the more socially nervous networker, the person who is almost always uncomfortable when first meeting strangers, the person who is nervous in crowds and the person who would rather be anywhere else than at a networking event.

Are you one of these people? Rest assured that you are not alone. Your problem is that you have to be networking as a key part of your marketing strategy and your business success. So, what can be done about this?

As a Master Practitioner of Neuro-linguistic Programming (NLP) I am a firm believer in and proponent of the simple yet extremely powerful behavioural attitude called "Acting as if."

As a simple description of a huge field of study, the early developers of NLP (Richard Bandler and John Grinder) closely studied several highly skilled individuals to distil the elements that they believed made them so skilled at what they did. Bandler and Grinder studied the physiology, attitudes, beliefs, language and behavioural strategies that their study participants used to achieve their outcomes. It turned out that when the distilled elements were used, in similar circumstances and by other practitioners, results were obtained that were similar in quality to the highly skilled study subjects. This technique became known as modelling.

The book you are reading is in essence all my networking knowledge, experience, passion, attitudes, physiology, beliefs and behavioural strategies distilled into these words and pages. It is a model of how I and other successful networkers actually network. You can take on and use these elements for yourself.

It sounds almost ridiculously easy but if you apply all the tips and techniques I have provided for you then, and this is the key part of the technique, couple them with the strong belief that you are a confident experienced networker, you will then be acting and behaving as if you are an experienced, confident and highly successful networker.

No one else will be able to tell that you are actually nervous and uncertain.

Within a short space of time you will find that you are an experienced and successful networker. This is the beauty of this method. You are not lying or conning anyone about anything. You are not claiming to be able to do something for someone else and charging them for it. You are simply eliminating all the usual time you might spend worrying about things that you cannot control and doing what works for you right from the start until it becomes a habit for you.

An alternative way to look at this is to identify someone else you know who is highly effective and confident at business networking; someone you would like to model or copy.

If you adopted their networking mannerisms, attitudes, techniques and behaviours and conducted your own networking in this way you would expect to be as successful as they are. You would be acting as if you were like them whilst networking.

You will always be you and you should not try to be anyone else. You can however act as if you can do what you want to do for yourself by having the attitude that you can actually do it for yourself.

Who do you know to be a top class networker and someone you could learn from, copy and model?

Try it and you might be amazed at what you can accomplish.

Your next steps

You have covered a lot of ground in reading this far. I hope I have challenged you and enlightened you regarding your view of business networking.

Remember that business networking is ultimately just a tool. It is in fact merely one tool of the many available to you as a marketer of your business. Whatever business you may think you are in you are also very definitely in the marketing business. When used well, networking is a powerful and enjoyable way to build your business and your success.

As discussed earlier, networking is not a theoretical activity. Networking is something you do. You can of course pick up hints, tips and strategies in a book like this but you will not develop yourself fully on theory alone. Thinking about networking is not networking. Talking about networking is not networking. Dreaming about networking is not networking. Networking is networking.

Take action and put the ideas and strategies you have learned or rediscovered into practice in the real world with real people. Discomfort is normal. It is a sign of growth. If you are uncomfortable you are growing. Stretch yourself and you might be amazed at all you can accomplish.

Attend business events, talk to people socially, try out and select a networking group, book a meeting and go networking.

Take the time to fully understand your business and the beneficial results it offers to others. Hone your dynamic introduction and repertoire of stories. Be memorable and passionate. Use powerful questions and language. Following up is all important so make sure you do it effectively. Develop good habits and constantly strive to improve and learn. Keep challenging the status quo and asking why. Have a positive mind-set and associate with positive people whenever you can. Smile often and brightly.

Remember above all things to have fun in everything you do in your life and work otherwise what is the point of it all?

This is the end of Business Networking for the Bewildered. I hope you have enjoyed reading it as much as I have enjoyed writing it.

Appendix

There is a virtual appendix of resources at: www.eryrglas.com/nwftbappendix

This page contains a number of useful free downloadable PDF checklists and pro-forma documents that you can use to help you on your networking journey. I will also use this page to post any significant book updates and other useful networking information.

You will also be able to sign up for my bi-monthly free newsletter to stay informed about other books, new services and new home study training materials as they are released.

About the author

Andy Pope is a professional speaker, speaker coach, communication consultant, trainer, networker and writer based in the UK.

Andy has real passion and enthusiasm for helping people to improve their face to face communication and interpersonal skills. First class communication skills are vital in the noisy business world of today and getting your message across clearly and effectively can mean the difference between you succeeding or failing.

For more information on the growing range of services, presentations, seminars, workshops and coaching options that are available for both individuals and organisations please visit his website at www.eryrglas.com or email him at networkingbook@eryrglas.com

CPSIA information can be obtained at www.ICGtesting.com
Printed in the USA
BVOW04s1003200115

384098BV00025B/251/P